Hebrews

Books in the Bible Study Commentary Series

Genesis—Leon J. Wood
Exodus—F. B. Huey, Jr.
Leviticus—Louis Goldberg
Numbers—F. B. Huey, Jr.
Deuteronomy—Louis Goldberg
Joshua—Paul P. Enns
Judges—Paul P. Enns
Ruth—Paul P. Enns
1, 2 Samuel—Howard F. Vos
1 2 Kings—Howard F. Vos
1, 2 Chronicles—Eugene H. Merrill
Ezra, Nehemiah, Esther—Howard F. Vos
Job—D. David Garland
**Psalms*— Ronald B. Allen
Proverbs—Eldon Woodcock
Ecclesiastes—Louis Goldberg
Song of Songs—Edward M. Curtis
Isaiah—D. David Garland
Jeremiah—F. B. Huey, Jr.
Lamentations—Dan G. Kent
Ezekiel—Paul P. Enns
Daniel—Leon J. Wood
Hosea—D. David Garland
Joel—Ronald B. Allen
Amos—D. David Garland
Obadiah, Jonah—John H. Walton and Bryan E. Beyer
Micah—Jack R. Riggs
Nahum, Habakkuk, Zephaniah, Haggai—J. N. Boo Heflin
Zechariah—Homer Heater, Jr.
Malachi—Charles D. Isbell
Matthew—Howard F. Vos
Mark—Howard F. Vos
Luke—Virtus E. Gideon
John—Herschel H. Hobbs
Acts—Curtis Vaughan
Romans—Curtis Vaughan and Bruce Corley
1 Corinthians—Curtis Vaughan and Thomas D. Lea
2 Corinthians—Aída B. Spencer and William D. Spencer
Galatians—Curtis Vaughan
Ephesians—Curtis Vaughan
Philippians—Howard F. Vos
Colossians and Philemon—Curtis Vaughan
The Thessalonian Epistles—John F. Walvoord
The Pastoral Epistles—E. M. Blaiklock
Hebrews—Leon Morris
James—Curtis Vaughan
1, 2 Peter, Jude—Curtis Vaughan and Thomas D. Lea
1, 2, 3 John—Curtis Vaughan
Revelation—Alan F. Johnson

*Not yet published as of this printing.

BIBLE STUDY COMMENTARY

Hebrews

LEON MORRIS

HEBREWS: BIBLE STUDY COMMENTARY

Lamplighter Books are published by Zondervan
Publishing House, 1415 Lake Drive, S.E.,
Grand Rapids, Michigan 49506

Library of Congress Cataloging in Publication Data

Morris, Leon, 1914–
Hebrews: Bible study commentary.
Bibliography: p.
1. Bible. N.T. Hebrews—Commentaries. I. Title.
BS2775.3.M67 1983 227'.8707 83-10251
ISBN 0-310-45183-3

Edited by Ed van der Maas

Printed in the United States of America

90 91 92 93 94 95 / EP / 9 8 7 6 5

Abbreviations

JB	Jerusalem Bible
KJV	King James Version
NEB	New English Bible
NIV	New International Version
RSV	Revised Standard Version
TEV	Today's English Version

Contents

Hebrews

Introductory Matters

A. Author

This writing is anonymous, and though there have been many attempts to identify the author, none of them can be said to have been successful. Christians have often agreed with Clement of Alexandria's suggestion that Paul wrote it, but there seems to be no real evidence for this view and much that speaks against it: the elegant Greek is unlike that of Paul (whose style is forceful and rugged), and the subject matter, with its emphasis on the tabernacle, the priesthood, the sacrifices, and Jewish liturgical concerns generally, differs from that of any of Paul's letters. Some suggest Barnabas, the principal support being that he was a Levite (Acts 4:36) and that the epistle contains much that would be of special interest to a Levite. But the writer says that the message of salvation was "confirmed to us by those who heard [the Lord]" (2:3), which Barnabas is unlikely to have written, since he probably heard Jesus himself. Other suggestions include Apollos, an eloquent man well-grounded in the Scriptures (Acts 18:24); he remains a possibility, but the evidence cannot be said to be impressive. Some have thought of Priscilla, who was knowledgeable enough to instruct Apollos (Acts 18:26); they point out that her being a woman would be a reason for the suppression of the author's name.

Such speculation is interesting. But in the end we are reduced to saying that we do not know. In any case, what is in the writing is more important than who wrote it.

B. Date

Some minor indications of the date of Hebrews are the mention of Timothy (13:23), which places it in the time of the early church, and the statement, "you have not yet resisted to the point of shedding your blood" (12:4), which points to a date before the persecutions, or at least before the lives of any of the community to which the letter was written had been lost in the persecutions. But the principal indication is the absence of any mention of the fall of Jerusalem and the destruction of the temple (A.D. 70). The author's argument that the sacrifices of the old way have no relevance now that Christ has offered His sacrifice would invite a reference to the cessation of those sacrifices if the temple and all that went with it had indeed ceased to exist. Perhaps the epistle was written during the war of A.D. 66–70, when loyal Jews everywhere would be sympathizing with the heroes fighting against Rome and any Jew would feel a strong urge to affirm his Jewishness.

C. Recipients

Traditionally it has been held that the letter was written to a group of Jewish Christians, perhaps a small group because they ought to have been teachers (5:12) and not many are teachers in any church. They were evidently being tempted to abandon the Christian way, for the writer warns against drifting away (2:1; 3:12; 4:1, 11; 6:4–6, 11–12, etc.), and the thrust of much of his argument is that the Christian way is God's final way. The consistent appeal to the Old Testament and to Levitical symbolism points to Jewish recipients, as do incidental references to "Abraham's descendants" (2:16) and to Jesus' superiority to Moses (3:1ff.). Some have thought that the letter was sent to a group of Jewish priests or perhaps to some members of the Qumran community. But such views are no more than speculation and seem ruled out by the fact that the recipients were certainly Christians (3:1; 6:9; 10:23).

Some have argued for a gentile destination, pointing to the elegant Greek and the use of the Septuagint, the Greek translation of the Old Testament. But this kind of reasoning proves little, for many educated Jews wrote excellent Greek and the Septuagint was a translation made so that Jews could read their Bible in a language they understood. Moreover, the constant appeal to the Old Testament speaks against this view: this would be of no avail if the readers were tempted to relapse into paganism, but if they were in danger of reverting to Judaism the Old Testament would still be sacred Scripture for them.

It seems that we cannot get far with such speculations. The subject matter of the letter makes it probable that the recipients were Jewish Christians; this is supported by the fact that the title "To Hebrews" is in the oldest manuscripts, and there is no evidence that it was ever missing. We should accept an original Jewish destination, but there is nothing more we can say with confidence. We simply do not know whether these Jewish Christians were in Palestine, Rome, or elsewhere.

D. Literary Form

We generally call this writing an "epistle," i.e., a letter, but this may not be correct. It is unlike any epistle in the New Testament (though in some ways it resembles 1 John). A first-century letter began with the writer's name, followed by the name of the recipients and a greeting, but this is not the way Hebrews begins. Some think it is a sermon, and the writer, indeed, calls it "my word of exhortation" (13:22; a sermon is described like this in Acts 13:15). The content makes it not improbable that it is based on a sermon, but as it stands the book is addressed to a definite small group: the readers ought to be teachers (5:12); the writer thinks highly of them (6:9) and is looking forward to seeing them (13:19, 23); he asks them to pray for him and he gives them news of Timothy (13:18, 23). Touches like this justify our calling the writing a letter, though it is not written in the normal form of a first-century letter.

E. The Use of the Old Testament

It is not surprising that the writer makes a good deal of use of the Old Testament, which was sacred Scripture for him as for the rest of the early church. But he has an individual approach. He concentrates largely on the Pentateuch and the Psalms: twenty-three of his twenty-nine quotations come from these two sections of the Old Testament. He uses the Septuagint almost exclusively.

He brings out the divine origin of Scripture by an unusual method of quotation. Normally he ascribes the passages he quotes directly to God and does not mention the human author. There are some exceptions (e.g., 4:7; 9:19–20), but the usage is striking. Sometimes he speaks of Christ as the author (2:11–12), and sometimes of the Holy Spirit (3:7; 10:15). It is quite plain that for this author, what Scripture says is indeed from God.

We should notice further that the writer sees the whole Old Testament as pointing forward to Christ, who is the fulfillment of all that the ancient Scripture says. He rejects Judaism because it does not see the meaning of its own Bible. It is only in Jesus that we see the meaning of the Old Testament as well as that of the New.

F. Outline

I. Introduction (1:1–4)
II. The Excellence of the Christ (1:5–3:6)
  A. Superior to the Angels (1:5–14)
  B. The Author of "Such a Great Salvation" (2:1–9)
  C. True Man (2:10–18)
  D. Superior to Moses (3:1–6)
III. The Promised Rest (3:7–4:13)
  A. Scriptural Basis (3:7–11)
  B. Some Did Not Enter the Rest (3:12–19)
  C. Christians Enter the Rest (4:1–10)
  D. Exhortation to Enter the Rest (4:11–13)

IV. A Great High Priest (4:14–5:11)
   A. Our Confidence (4:14–16)
   B. The Qualities Required in High Priests (5:1–4)
   C. Christ's Qualifications as High Priest (5:5–11)
V. The Danger of Apostasy (5:12–6:20)
   A. Failure to Progress in the Faith (5:12–14)
   B. Exhortation to Progress (6:1–3)
   C. No Second Beginning (6:4–8)
   D. Exhortation to Perseverance (6:9–12)
   E. God's Promise Is Sure (6:13–20)
VI. A Priest Like Melchizedek (7:1–28)
   A. The Greatness of Melchizedek (7:1–10)
   B. The Royal Priesthood of Melchizedek and of Christ (7:11–14)
   C. Christ's Priesthood Is Superior (7:15–28)
VII. A New and Better Covenant (I) (8:1–9:28)
   A. Christ's "More Excellent" Ministry (8:1–7)
   B. The Old Covenant Superseded (8:8–13)
   C. The Old Sanctuary and Its Ritual (9:1–10)
   D. The Blood of Christ (9:11–14)
   E. The Mediator of the New Covenant (9:15–22)
   F. The Perfect Sacrifice (9:23–28)
VIII. A New and Better Covenant (II) (10:1–39)
   A. The Law a Shadow (10:1–4)
   B. One Sacrifice for Sins (10:5–18)
   C. The Sequel—The Right Way (10:19–25)
   D. The Sequel—The Wrong Way (10:26–31)
   E. Choose the Right Way (10:32–39)
IX. Faith (11:1–40)
   A. The Meaning of Faith (11:1–3)
   B. The Faith of the Men Before the Flood (11:4–7)
   C. The Faith of Abraham and Sarah (11:8–19)
   D. The Faith of the Patriarchs (11:20–22)
   E. The Faith of Moses (11:23–28)
   F. The Faith of the Exodus Generation (11:29–31)
   G. The Faith of Other Servants of God (11:32–38)
   H. The Promise (11:39–40)
X. Christian Living (12:1–13:19)
   A. Christ Our Example (12:1–3)
   B. Discipline (12:4–11)
   C. Exhortation to Live the Christian Life (12:12–17)
   D. Mount Sinai and Mount Zion (12:18–24)
   E. A Kingdom That Cannot Be Shaken (12:25–29)
   F. Love (13:1–6)
   G. Christian Leadership (13:7–8)

- H. Christian Sacrifice (13:9–16)
- I. Christian Obedience (13:17)
- J. Prayer (13:18–19)

XI. Conclusion (13:20–25)
- A. Doxology (13:20–21)
- B. Final Exhortations (13:22–25)

Chapter 1

Introduction

(Hebrews 1:1–4)

Jesus is a wonderful Savior. He is infinitely greater than the greatest of created beings. He died to bring about a wonderful salvation, a salvation adequate for the needs of all mankind. These tremendous truths gripped the author of this letter and he dwells on them lovingly. His opening is a majestic sentence in which he shows that Jesus is greater than the prophets and that He has a special relationship to God. He took part in creation and in due course He accomplished the purification of men from their sins. He is greater by far than any angel. This forms a magnificent introduction to a magnificent theme.

In the opening verse we are reminded that God has been active in revelation from very early times ("in the past" means "in olden days" rather than "recently"). God spoke to "our forefathers," an expression that is often used of the great patriarchs but that here means God's people in Old Testament days. The term is broad enough to cover all to whom the revelation came. It was God who spoke and He spoke "through," or more exactly "in" the prophets. It is true that God's word came "through" these great men. They did not put forward their own ideas but the message God had given them. It is also true that God was "in" them. Both thoughts are present.

God brought the revelation to the prophets "in various ways." Sometimes He did it through dreams (Dan. 7:1; He might even speak to the heathen in this way, Dan. 2:3). Sometimes there was a vision, as in Ezekiel's case (Ezek. 8:4; 11:24). Or God might use ordinary objects like the basket of ripe fruit that Amos saw and through which God's word came to him (Amos 8:1). Similarly, Jeremiah received a message from God when he saw "the branch of an almond tree" (Jer. 1:11). "The hand of the Lord came upon Elisha" on one occasion while a "harpist was playing" (2 Kings 3:15). Not infrequently an angel brought the Lord's message (e.g., Zech. 1:9). And there are still other ways. God spoke to Adam and Eve (Gen. 3), to Abram (Gen. 12:1), and especially to Moses (Exod. 3:4, etc.). Our author is clear about both the variety of God's ways of speaking to people and the long period during which He had been doing this. He spoke to men throughout Old Testament times down to the time of Malachi (Mal. 1:1).

But now something even more wonderful has happened: "in these last days he has spoken to us by his Son" (v. 2). The writer is saying more than that Jesus was the last in a long line of prophets and other holy men. He is not merely a prophet, He is God's "Son." He stands in a different relationship to God and to man. It is His essential nature to be "Son," whereas theirs was to be "prophet." They belonged with men; He belongs with God. There is, of course, a sense in which He belongs with men, too, for He really became man; our author will bring that out later. Here his point is that Jesus is the culmination of the revelation from God. He does not use the expression "Messiah," but this is essentially what he is saying. Jesus has brought about a new state of affairs, the Messianic Age. He is thus greater by far than any of those who in earlier days had been the recipients of revelation.

There is another important point. We could translate the opening words in this way: "God, having spoken in the prophets . . . has spoken in One who is Son." It is the same God who spoke in the prophets who is now speaking in the Son. There is a continuity with the old revelation. The prophets were not discarded when the Son came. The Old Testament remains sacred Scripture for the followers of Jesus. The revelation made in Jesus Christ is the culmination of the revelation made in Old Testament days, but it does not repudiate that revelation. It is continuous with it, it presupposes it. Our author will bring this out again and again by his references to the Old Testament and to the fulfillments of its prophecies in the person and the work of Jesus. We must overlook neither the continuity between the prophets and Jesus nor the discontinuity brought about by the fact that He is the Messiah who ushered in the Messianic Age, while they were no more than its heralds. Throughout this epistle the writer is concerned that the Christian way is God's final way. There must be no going back from it.

Now come eight important statements about the Son.

1. *He is "heir of all things"* (v. 2)

The verb "appointed" is perhaps unexpected. The writer might have said simply that Jesus "is" heir. Some see a reference here to a specific event such as the ascension of Christ, but the sense "designated in advance" (Héning; cf. also Ps. 2:7, quoted in v. 5) seems better. In any case, the emphasis here is on "heir" rather than on "appointed." The word "heir" often denotes one who possesses property on the death of the previous owner, but in the New Testament it is often used of firm possession, no matter how the possession took place. Here it points to the dignity and the greatness of Christ. In a great estate there was no one so important as the heir; he had a dignity superior to that of anyone else. The writer is saying that Christ has the dignity of "heir" in all this mighty universe. He is in the position of Son of the Owner. He has the highest place (cf. Phil. 2:9–11; Col. 1:15).

2. *Through Him God "made the universe"* (v. 2)

The New Testament sees God, of course, as the Creator of all things. We are not to think of a number of different creators. But God created "through" His Son, a truth we find in a number of places (John 1:3; 1 Cor. 8:6; Col. 1:16). To think of Him as involved in the creation of all that is, is to think of Him as supremely great. The term translated "the universe" is literally "the ages." Some think that it should be understood in a temporal sense: God through Christ created all the "times" there are. Others remind us that the word is also used in the sense of "world" but take the plural strictly and understand it to mean "the worlds" (KJV). Christ was instrumental in the creation of whatever worlds there are. Whichever way we take it, we are assured that Christ was involved in the creation of everything that exists.

3. *"The Son is the radiance of God's glory"* (v. 3)

This plainly means that the Son is closely connected with God's glory, but there is dispute as to precisely how. The word translated "radiance" may mean the shining forth of brightness, or it may mean the reflection of brightness. If we take the first meaning, the writer is saying that God's glory shines out from Christ. That glory is, so to speak, in Him. If we take the second (as Goodspeed does, "the reflection of God's glory"), then there is a glory of God that Christ reflects to us. The former is to be preferred, but either way we are being told that the glory of God is to be seen in Christ. Glory is associated with the presence of God (e.g., Ezek. 1:28; 11:23; cf. also John 1:14).

4. *"The exact representation of his being"* (v. 3)

The Greek word *charaktēr*, "exact representation," is found only here in the New Testament. It was used of a mark stamped on something, for example, on metal in the making of coins (which is behind the translation of the RSV, "the very stamp of his nature"). Every coin stamped by the same die is, of course, exactly like every other, and this is the point of choosing this word. The Son shows us exactly what God is. We are not left to wonder. Jesus Christ has shown us. "Being" points to essential nature. Christ reveals what God really is and not just some minor aspect.

5. *"Sustaining all things by his powerful word"* (v. 3)

The Son was God's agent in the work of creation (v. 2); now we learn that He did not, so to speak, take His hands off creation once the universe was made. He keeps it going. It is due to the Son's presence that the created universe continues to exist and does not simply disintegrate. The thought seems also present that He is carrying it along, bearing it toward an important goal. Creation is not aimless: it is part of God's plan and the Son is continually bearing creation along toward the fulfillment of that plan. To do all this He needs only "his powerful word." We read later that "the universe was formed at God's command" (11:3), where "command" translates the same word as that used here. Our author is in no doubt about its effectiveness. God called everything into existence simply by His word (cf. the repeated "And God said" in Gen. 1). And now we learn that it is by Christ's powerful word that everything is upheld and carried along to the goal for which it was intended.

6. *He "provided purification for sins"* (v. 3)

"Provided" is the usual word for "made" and simply means that the purification was brought about. The general term does not specify *how* this was done; the emphasis is on *what* was done, and that was purification, the cleansing away of sins. At the same time we should notice that the tense of the verb indicates that the action is complete. Christ has fully performed the purification. Nothing needs to be added to what He did at Calvary. Sin may be viewed in a number of ways: it is a missing of the mark, it is a going astray, it is a stumbling, it is rebellion against God. Here sin is seen as defiling; it makes the sinner unclean, unfit to be in the presence of a holy God. But Christ did all that was necessary to take away the defilement. Now the sinner can stand before God as one who has been cleansed.

The word "sin" occurs twenty-five times in this epistle, more often than in any other New Testament book except Romans (forty-eight times). The frequency with which the writer refers to it shows that he sees sin as the great barrier between God and man. He writes in the glad certainty that this barrier has been demolished. Christ has opened up the way to God by taking our sin out of the way. There are many ways in which he sees Christ to have done this. Christ made propitiation for our sins (2:17), offered a sacrifice for sins (10:12), did away with sin (9:26), bore sin (9:28). Because of what He has done there is no longer a sacrifice for sin (10:18). Sins have been forgiven (10:18), God remembers them no more (10:17). Christ's death is a ransom to set people free from sins (even those committed in Old Testament days, 9:15). By contrast, the older way could not deal with sin (10:1–2, 4, 6, 11). Clearly the writer sees the salvation Christ brought about as many-sided. Look at sin how you will, the Son has dealt with it.

7. *He is seated at God's right hand* (v. 3)

The older writers delighted to speak of "the finished work of Christ," and it is this that finds expression here. All our language about heaven is necessarily symbolic. We have not been there yet and we have no words to say exactly what it is like. But the words we use point to important truths. Thus, sitting is the position of rest and God's right hand is the place of honor. The writer is saying that Christ's saving work is done (He is seated) and that it is accepted in the highest possible place (since He is in the place of highest honor at God's right hand, God approves of what He has done). When a priest is at work he is standing (10:11), but the saving work of Christ, our great high priest, is over. We should perhaps notice a Jewish idea that the angels stand (they do not sit) in the presence of God (cf. v. 13). That the Son is not only seated, but is seated at the right hand, indicates that He is in a position far superior to that of any angel.

"The Majesty" is an unusual way of referring to God (it is used of God only here and in 8:1 in the whole New Testament). The word properly means "greatness," from which it is a short step to "majesty." When he thinks of Christ's work as finished, the writer thinks of God in all His greatness as having accepted it.

8. *He is "superior to the angels"* (v. 4)

We have seen that the Son's superiority to the angels is implied in His sitting at God's right hand. Now we see also that His "name" marks Him out as superior to them. In antiquity, a name meant a good deal more than it does to us. For us a name is little more than a label, a way of distinguishing one from another. But in the world of the New Testament the name stood for the whole person, it summed up all he was (cf. Rev. 2:17, where a person receives a new name which no one else knows; from our point of view that is useless, but in antiquity it conveyed the precious truth that God was giving the person a new character, and this was a secret between God and him). So the "name" of the Son is such that He is superior to the angels.

It is unexpected that He "became superior (cf. "appointed," v. 2). We might have anticipated a statement that He was always superior to the angels, and indeed, what has been said about Him makes it clear that this is so. But at this point our author carries on the thought that Christ has brought salvation to men: His finished work of salvation shows Him to be superior to angels. None of them can be known as "Savior." Their work is to be "ministering spirits" (v. 14), His is to be the Savior of all God's people.

The NIV uses "superior" twice in this verse, but they are two different Greek words (cf. KJV). The first means "better" and is usually translated so. It is a favorite word of the author, who uses it thirteen times out of its nineteen New Testament occurrences. It is one of his major thoughts that the Christian way is "better": it deals with better things (6:9), a better hope (7:19), a better covenant (7:22; 8:6), better promises (8:6), better sacrifices (9:23), a better possession (10:34), a better country (11:16), a better resurrection (11:35), something better (11:40), and blood that speaks better (12:24). We should not miss his strong emphasis that the Christian way is superior to every other way: it is God's final answer to the problem of man's sin and as such it is superior to every human system. It accords with this that the Savior is "better" than any angel.

The other word for "superior" means "more excellent." The Son's name far surpasses any other name. This name is "inherited," which is again somewhat surprising. We might have thought of the name as something He always had. But there is no question of someone dying and of His thus obtaining possession of the name; rather, the thought is of secure possession (cf. "heir" in v. 2). That name is His and it is rightly His. The writer does not say what this name is. It may be a name people do not know (cf. Rev. 19:12), or it may be "Son" (v. 2).

This general survey of the person and the work of Christ has brought out His relationship to the Father, His preexistence, His place in bringing about and in sustaining creation, His incarnation, His atoning work, and His return to glory. It is a great deal to pack into one Greek sentence, and it forms a magnificent picture of a magnificent Savior that serves to introduce the reader to some of the important thoughts that will recur throughout the epistle.

For Further Study

1. Make a list of all the things you can learn about Christ from these verses.
2. Look up the passages where the writer uses the word "better." What do they tell you about the Christian way?
3. What do these verses teach us about God?

Chapter 2

The Excellence of the Christ

(Hebrews 1:5–3:6)

The first stage in the argument is a demonstration of the superiority of Christ to the angels. This has already been shown briefly in the introduction, but the writer proceeds to bring out the point in greater detail by showing that the Scriptures of the Old Testament bear witness to this truth. It is important to see that Christ is not simply another prophet, another great man of God. He is far superior to all men, which becomes obvious when it is seen that He is superior even to angels. This does not mean that He was not a true man. No one insists more strongly on the genuine humanity of Jesus than this writer does—it is central to his argument that the One who is so high really came where we are. How else could He have died for our salvation? But at this point his concern is with the greatness of the Son. No angel can compare with Him.

A. Superior to the Angels (1:5–14)

This passage contains seven quotations from the Old Testament, five of which are from the Psalms. The first is from Psalm 2:7, which does not explicitly mention the Christ. But our author clearly sees the whole Old Testament as bearing witness to Christ and this psalm as messianic. He sees it as especially significant that the term "my Son" is used. Angels are in fact occasionally called "sons of God" (see NIV mg. of Job 1:6; 2:1), and Israel God's "son" (Exod. 4:22; Hos. 11:1; so also Ephraim, Jer. 31:9). God promised that Solomon would be His "son" (2 Sam. 7:14). But none of these passages is really like Psalm 2: none sets one individual apart to stand in a relationship to God that is unique in all creation. That is the writer's point. Jesus Christ is "Son" in a way that no one else is. The question to what "today" refers is probably unanswerable. The writer is quoting the psalm, and since he found the word there he included it here. But he makes nothing of it and clearly he does not think of a special day on which Jesus became God's Son. He always was the Son, and while the psalmist may well have had some special day in mind, this is not the concern of the writer of this epistle.

He adds words from 2 Samuel 7:14 (=1 Chron. 17:13). They were used originally of Solomon, but, as in the case of the previous quotation, the writer sees a fuller meaning in them. They are messianic and tell us something about the Messiah as well as about Solomon. It is important that the Messiah stands to God in the relation of Son to Father. This is something that cannot be said of any angel and sets Christ apart from them all.

The reference to God's bringing the firstborn into the world (v. 6) has been seen by some as referring to the Incarnation, by others to the Second Coming. But there is no indication that the writer had either specifically in mind. It is more likely that he is thinking of the Son as sovereign over all there is without any emphasis on a particular historical event. It is His supreme place that is in mind rather than the time of its manifestation. The quotation brings out the one point that the angels worship Him. There is no other of whom this can be said. The words do not occur in the Hebrew of Deuteronomy 32:43, but the expression "sons of God" is found in the Septuagint (the translation into Greek) of that verse and "angels" occurs later in the same verse.[1] The writer thus gives us the sense of it. We should not overlook the word "all"; the worship of all heaven is accorded to the Son.

What then of the angels? Part of the answer is found in Psalm 104:4. The Hebrew of this verse can be understood in the sense of the NIV translation: "He makes winds his messengers, flames of fire his servants." But it is also possible to take it in the sense of the Septuagint, which our author quotes: "God makes his messengers [= angels] winds. . . ." This means that they are as swift as the wind, as powerful as flames of fire. It puts the angels in a special place. But, high though this place is above the place of men, it is far below that of the Son. Wind and fire are part of creation, but He is not.

Attention turns back to the Son with a quotation from Psalm 45:6, 7 (vv. 8–9). Originally the psalm referred to a royal wedding, but as in the case of other passages, our author sees the psalm as messianic. Beyond the reference to the king of Israel there is a fuller reference to the Messiah. This passage emphasizes the sovereignty and eternity of the Messiah. Notice His throne, His scepter, His kingdom, and His being set above His companions. His eternity is conveyed in the words "will last for ever and ever." There is a concern for moral values in the repeated references to righteousness. It is possible to take the first "God" in verse 9 as an address; "Therefore O God, your God has set you . . . ," in which case the Messiah is twice addressed as God in this passage. What was only

[1]In the Septuagint, Deuteronomy 32:43 reads, "Rejoice, O heavens, with him, and let all the sons of God worship him; rejoice, O nations, with his people, and let all the angels of God strengthen themselves in him."

symbolically applicable to the Davidic king is true in the fullest sense of the Messiah. Anointing was an action that solemnly set someone apart for a sacred function (e.g., Exod. 28:41; 1 Kings 19:16). The Messiah is thus solemnly set above all others. Who are His "companions"? Probably those whom Jesus is not ashamed to call "brothers" (2:11) (the word rendered "companions" here is also used in 3:14, where it is translated as a verb, "to share"). We should not miss the note of joy with which the verse ends. Joy runs through the New Testament and is an integral part of the Christian way.

Next the writer turns to Christ's eternity (v. 10), which he brings out in contrast with created things (quoting Ps. 102:25–27). It tells us something of his view of Christ that he takes words that in the Old Testament refer to God and applies them to Christ. What is true of the One is true of the Other. We have already seen that the Son was God's agent in creation (v. 2), and we come back to this thought with His laying the foundations of the earth and His making of the heavens. But the point is not so much that He is great enough to create, but that creation will pass away while He, by contrast, remains eternally (vv. 11–12). Heaven and earth appear to us to be lasting and solid. But they will wear out like clothes do; the process takes a little longer but it is just as certain. In the end heaven and earth will disappear and be replaced with something else (Isa. 66:22; Rev. 6:14; 21:1). But not so the Son: to Him it may be said, "you remain the same, and your years will never end."

The final quotation (from Ps. 110:1) brings out the superiority of the Son by showing that what it says of Him is totally inapplicable to the angels. This psalm was widely accepted as messianic and it brings out the greatness of the Messiah by referring to His being seated at God's right hand (see comments on v. 3) and to the complete destruction of His enemies. We have already noted that the angels stand before God, but the Messiah, the Son, is different. The difference is brought out with the completely unexpected picture of God acting like a servant as He makes Messiah's enemies into a footstool! This, of course, means that He renders them completely powerless. The picture is that of the total triumph of the Messiah, a concept we cannot apply to any angel.

All the angels ("all" means that there is no exception) are servants in one way or another (v. 14). "Spirits" is a reminder that they are on a different level from us, but "ministering" means that their task is service. It is both humbling and inspiring that God means the angels to serve, not only Him but also us, "who will inherit salvation." The word "inherit," strictly speaking, means to obtain something as a result of the death of someone who bequeaths it to us. But in the New Testament it is often used simply of sure possession, without regard to the means whereby the possession is obtained (cf. comments on vv. 2, 4). In a place such as this there may be a glance at the fact that it was the death of Christ that brought us our possession, but it is no more than a glance, for He is no longer dead but alive. What is emphasized is that salvation is a sure possession.

The word "salvation" is found seven times in Hebrews, which is more than in any other New Testament book. It is an important concept for our author. In itself the word can mean all kinds of deliverance, but in the New Testament it is the deliverance Christ has wrought for us. It is the comprehensive term of which justification, sanctification, and the like are aspects. The term may be used of the deliverance that we have already received in Christ, or it may look forward to the consummation of that deliverance when Christ returns. The future tense shows that the emphasis here is on what will happen when He comes again.

B. The Author of "Such a Great Salvation" (2:1–9)

The writer proceeds to bring out the greatness of Jesus by referring to the great salvation He brought about. The author of a salvation valid "for everyone" (2:9) must be infinitely great. This stage of the argument begins with a warning not to fall away. "Therefore" (v. 1) is a significant link with the preceding: the Son is greatly superior to the angels, *therefore* it is important to take careful notice of Him. We must pay attention "to what we have heard," an expression the writer does not explain, but which clearly means the gospel, the message of what Christ has done. His use of "we" shows that he is not one of the original disciples. He, as well as his readers, was included in the number of those who had heard the gospel. Having heard it and accepted it, he now sees it as something too valuable to be lost. He warns his readers not to "drift away" from it. It is not necessary to be an open and notorious sinner to be lost. That can be accomplished by quietly drifting away.

The writer contrasts the gospel with the Old Testament way by a reference to their respective origins. "The message spoken by angels" (v. 2) is the Law given on Sinai, the message that all faithful Jews accepted without question as God's greatest gift to mankind. There is nothing in the Old Testament about angels being involved in the giving of the Law (though it is mentioned in the Septuagint, Deut. 33:2), but it is attested in some New Testament passages (Acts 7:53; Gal. 3:19) and is mentioned by the Jewish historian Josephus and in some rabbinic passages. The presence of angels on that great occasion was thus well known. Incidentally, it is more correct to read "through angels" than "by angels." The writer is not saying that the angels originated the Law, for he clearly accepts God as its author. But God gave it to Israel "through" angels. In Judaism this was held to show its great dignity and value; it was far superior to anything that was linked only to human activity. But our author uses the angels to prove inferiority: what came through angels could not compare in value with that which came through the Son. That does not mean any belittlement of the Law. It was "binding." Everything in it came from God. Angels, God's messengers, had graced its introduction to the world of men. Thus it had to be kept and people could look only for "just punishment" for every act of disobedience.

If this is true of the Law (which was inferior to the gospel), then what are we to say of the gospel? The writer poses an unanswerable question when he asks, "how shall we escape if we ignore such a great salvation?" (v. 3). His word for "we" is emphatic, a construction he uses sparingly (five times only in all his epistle). This means that it should be taken seriously on the few occasions it occurs. Its force is that *we*, with our great privilege of having the gospel, *we* in contrast to those who know nothing more than the Law, *we* must not expect that God will take it calmly if we do nothing about the gospel. It cost Him the life of His Son and shall we simply neglect it? Notice that, as in verse 1, it is not a matter of open and blatant opposition, but simply one of neglect, of ignoring the great salvation. Anyone who does not accept God's offer of salvation does not receive God's salvation. It is as simple as that.

The fact that it is indeed a great salvation is brought out by three important facts.

1. *It was first proclaimed by the Lord* (cf. Luke 19:9)

Once again we should read "through" rather than "by"; the salvation in question originated with God and it was He who spoke of it through the Son. "The Lord" is a title not frequently used of Christ in Hebrews (though cf. 7:14; 13:20); in this letter it most often occurs in quotations from the Old Testament. But "the Lord" required no explanation in Christian circles. There was "but one Lord, Jesus Christ" (1 Cor. 8:6; cf. 1 Cor. 12:13), and anything He said must be listened to carefully.

2. *It was confirmed by those who heard Jesus*

From the beginning, the function of those who were with Jesus was important. Jesus chose the Twelve to be with Him and that He might send them out to preach (Mark 3:14; they were also to cast out demons). At a later time, after Judas had fallen away and someone was needed to replace him, the requirement was that he be "a witness" of the Resurrection (Acts 1:22). Christians must constantly appeal to the earliest testimony, for only that which agrees with what Jesus taught and did can be regarded as authentic. Our author makes it clear that the message he and his correspondents had received was the authentic message that was guaranteed by those who were close to Jesus and heard Him. The verb rendered "confirmed" was in frequent use as a technical legal term with a meaning similar to our "guarantee." It is a strong expression; there cannot be the slightest doubt about the message they have received. It has the fullest attestation; it is unconditionally guaranteed.

3. *God attested it* (v. 4)

Not only did the first preachers attest the message, but God bore witness with them. The fourth Gospel has the striking thought that God has borne witness to Jesus (John 5:37). God, so to speak, has gone on record that He has committed Himself in His Son. He has said and done what Jesus has said and done. If anything, the present passage is even more striking, for here we find that God has committed Himself in the preaching of the first Christian preachers. He bore witness with them (the Greek translated "testified" is actually a compound, "with-testified," i.e., God testified along with the people in question). He did this in various ways and the writer brings out something of this with his choice of different words for miracles and the like.

"Signs" is a word used often by John (but not by the Synoptists) for Jesus' miracles. It directs attention to the fact that the miracles were "significant" events. They were not simply inexplicable happenings beyond the powers of ordinary people. They had meaning. They pointed men to the truth of God. Those with spiritual perception would recognize that the miracles in question were not simply mind-boggling wonders but indications that God was at work; they were pointers, signposts to bring men to God. This does not mean that there was nothing "marvelous" about the miracles, and the writer goes on to refer to "wonders." The signs were such that they could not be explained. What comes from God is beyond man's understanding. Though it is not the most important aspect of the miracles, we should never dismiss the "wonder" aspect as though it signified nothing. The New Testament writers, it is true, never use it by itself when they are talking about the miracles, but it is not unimportant and so it is included here. With these go "various miracles," the word "various" denoting literally "many-colored." It points us to the truth that God's work is infinitely varied and beautiful. It has many colors, dark as well as bright, and is never monotonous. "Miracles" is a word common in the synoptic Gospels, where it means "mighty works," "deeds of power." Just as the first word in this little list pointed to the meaning and significance, so this one points to the mighty power involved. A miracle involves a power that men do not have. In conjunction with the preaching of the gospel it attests an important truth: the miracle means that a superhuman power is at work and the gospel it attests means that a superhuman power transforms people. To take sinners and make of them the saints of God is not a human achievement.

"Gifts of the Holy Spirit" is ambiguous. It may mean "gifts the Holy Spirit gives" (as in 1 Cor. 12:11) or "gifts of the Holy Spirit Himself" (as in Gal. 3:5; the plural would point to the gift of the Holy Spirit as given to many people). We probably should not make too sharp a distinction, for in fact God gave the gift and the gifts. The writer does not say what these gifts were; it is enough that the readers knew what they were and that they were from God. Whenever the Spirit is at work among men, God is at work and that is what matters. The readers could recognize that the gifts of the Spirit they knew so well were in fact an important testimony to the divine origin of the gospel. One more thing about the gifts is that they were distributed according to the will of God. They are never given just as men want. They originate with God and they go forth to accomplish God's purpose. They are never at men's disposal.

The writer turns from the first preaching and its attestation to the ultimate destiny of creation. "The world to come" is not subjected to angels (v. 5), though the language used implies that it is subjected to someone. From yet another point of view Christ's greatness and His superiority to the angels is brought out. The writer keeps insisting on this point.

He advances his argument with a quotation from Scripture (vv. 6–8), which he introduces with a verb used in this way only here in the New Testament. It has a meaning like "testify solemnly," which shows that he wants the words that follow to be taken with full seriousness. He does not say where the words come from (they come from Ps. 8:4–6), but simply says that "someone" has testified. This does not mean that he is not sure of the source; his quotation is exact and he clearly knows what he is doing. But for this writer the human author of Scripture is unimportant; all that matters is what God has said in the Bible. So he concentrates on the words and ignores both author and source. The passage he quotes combines a concern for both the smallness and the greatness of man. There is nothing in man to justify the fact that God is "mindful" of him. The thought in "mindful" is that when God remembers someone He helps him. Thus God remembered Noah and caused the flood to recede (Gen. 8:1); He remembered Abraham and delivered his nephew (Gen. 19:29); He remembered Rachel and she became pregnant (Gen. 30:22–23). As the verb is used in Scripture, "to be mindful" does not simply involve cerebral activity but a loving determination to assist. "The son of" is a Hebrew way of saying "characterized by." For example, in 1 Samuel 18:17, "serve me bravely" is more literally "be for me a son of valor" and in Jeremiah 48:45 the "noisy boasters" are "sons of noise." So here "the son of man" means much the same as "man" in the preceding line; the change is a matter of poetic parallelism. The psalmist sees nothing in man that would cause God to care for him. Yet the love of God is undoubted. The reason for it is surely not in man but in God Himself.

When the psalmist had made his point about the unimportance of man, he went on to show that this is not the only thing to be said. God in His love has set man in a position "a little lower than the angels." There is a slight uncertainty about the meaning of the words in the psalm. The NIV translates "a little lower than the heavenly beings" and has a marginal alternative, "a little lower than God." The writer of this epistle follows the

Septuagint and reads "the angels." Any one of these three can be defended, but whichever one we accept, the passage is saying that God has given man the supreme place here on earth (cf. Gen. 1:26–28), a place of both "glory" and "honor." If we look at God, man is very small and unimportant, but if we look at creation, man is in a glorious and honored place.

This is summed up in the words, "and put everything under his feet" (v. 8), which the writer proceeds to explain: "God left nothing that is not subject to him." Man is supreme. There is nothing here on earth that has a rightful supremacy over man. He has a very glorious and a very responsible position.

But that is not the way it all works out. What we see right now is far from everything being subject to man. Some of it is man's own fault. Thus, man cuts down trees and creates dustbowls and finds himself unable to handle the resultant situation. But it is not this that our author is thinking of so much as the frustrations that are built into life. For example, the medical man in one of the world's poorer countries knows that if he saves the life of his sick patient he is condemning someone else to die of hunger, for there is not enough food for all. Again, our physical strength is not great enough for us to accomplish all that we want to do. In every walk of life we meet frustration in one way or another. Everything is not subject to us, whether we are referring to individuals or to the race as a whole. This subjection is God's ultimate will for man, but "at present we do not see" it.

What we do see is Jesus (v. 9) and in Him we see the fulfillment, although in a way we would not have anticipated. Just as man is made a little lower than the angels, so it is with Him. But whereas for us this is the state God has assigned, for Him it was a place voluntarily assumed so that He "might taste death for everyone" ("taste death," of course, means "die"; cf. Luke 9:27, etc.). He came where we are with the definite purpose of dying for sinners. The result is that He is now "crowned with glory and honor," and the writer makes sure that we do not miss the connection by adding, "because he suffered death." Jesus lived a life like ours, with the frustrations and difficulties and opposition that we know so well (though, of course, He met them in a way that we should, but do not). But it was not this living the life that was the glory and the honor. That was rather the consequence of the atoning death that He died.

We find the human name Jesus nine times in this letter (here, 3:1; 4:14; 6:20; 7:22; 10:19; 12:2, 24; 13:12; "Jesus Christ" occurs three times, and "our Lord Jesus" once). The human name puts emphasis on the genuine humanity of the Savior. He was the man Jesus. The full humanity of our Lord is important for the author, and this emphasis on the human name is part of the way he brings it out.

C. True Man (2:10–18)

The author pursues his argument by enlarging on this thought of the genuine humanity of Jesus. It might be thought that this is a digression, that instead of carrying on with the thought of Jesus' greatness he now turns aside to speak of a different truth. But this would be a superficial understanding. He has spoken of a great Savior, greater than the angels, who produced a great salvation. Now he proceeds to show that in pursuit of this great aim Jesus stooped so low as to come down to where we are. To secure the salvation that was set before Him He was great enough to take the lowly path. The emphasis on the true humanity is an integral part of the author's argument concerning the excellence of the Christ.

This salvation is a process of "bringing many sons to glory" (v. 10). Left to ourselves we would probably not have thought of the bringing about of salvation as involving the incarnation of the Son of God. We tend to think in terms of palaces rather than of stables, of mighty conquerors rather than sufferers on crosses. But the writer makes the point that the way God chose was "fitting." God does not necessarily do things in the way we would like them done, but there is an inherent suitability about Christ's becoming man, living in lowliness and rejection, and then dying on a cross for our salvation. It accords with the God who is the Father of all His people, "for whom and through whom everything exists." It is His greatness that dictates the means He uses.

The writer speaks of Jesus as "the author of their salvation"; the word translated "author" may mean a leader ("captain," KJV), or someone who goes first ("pioneer," RSV). The word thus may emphasize authorship, leadership, or priority. It seems that "author" is the right word here, but the writer may also want us to see that Jesus went on ahead of us as He walked the way that led to the world's salvation.

The verse goes on to refer to Jesus as having been "made perfect." This is a surprising thought to those who are accustomed to seeing Him as the perfect example and it needs careful definition. But it is an important concept for our author, for he repeats it a number of times. The point is that there is more than one kind of perfection. There is, for example, one kind of perfection in the bud and another in the flower. It is one thing to be perfect in an elementary exercise and another to attain perfection at an advanced level. There is a perfection in having borne suffering rightfully, which is more than being perfectly ready to suffer if need be. Jesus always had the latter perfection but He attained the former in all its fullness only when He died on the cross.

The thoughts that He is "the author" of our salvation and that He suffered in this earthly life lead to the further thought that there is a profound unity between Jesus and His own. He is here called "the one who makes men holy" (v. 11), an idea to which the writer will come back (10:10). "Those who are made holy" comes, of course, from the same verb and indicates a link between Jesus and those He saves. This is emphasized by saying that they are all "of one" (NIV has "of the same family" but there is nothing corresponding to "family" in the Greek; this is apparently an inference from the references to "one" and to "brothers"). The meaning seems to be that Jesus shares our descent from Adam. He is a true member of the human race.

Because He has really come where we are He can call us "brothers." This way of speaking is not found often, and indeed, Jesus' relationship to the Father is so different from ours that He could say, "you have only one Master and you are all brothers" (Matt. 23:8), excluding Himself from the group of "brothers." The word is used of those in Jesus' immediate family (Luke 8:19–20), but sometimes also of those close to Him in a spiritual sense as when He said, "My mother and brothers are those who hear God's word and put it into practice" (Luke 8:21). What our author does here is thus not without parallel. There is a meaningful sense in which we are brothers of our Lord in the household of the Father. Characteristically, the writer backs this up with an appeal to Scripture. He quotes from Psalm 22:22, a psalm whose opening words Jesus quoted as He hung on the cross (Mark 15:34) and from which John derives a prophecy about the disposing of His clothing (John 19:24). There was thus no doubt in the early church that it applied to Jesus and it is accordingly significant that the speaker refers to "my brothers." Jesus stood in a close relationship to those for whom He died.

The "name" means all that the person is, and here it means that he declares to His "brothers" who and what the Father is. The thought is repeated in other words in the next line. "Congregation" was used of the assembly of Israel of old (often in the Greek Old Testament and sometimes in the New, e.g., Acts 7:38). It became the usual name for the church (as the KJV translates it here). The parallelism of the psalm makes it more or less synonymous with "my brothers" in the preceding line: the brothers of Jesus are the members of His church. There is a festal air about "sing your praises," so the quotation ends on the note of joy.

The writer proceeds to give us two more quotations. There are a couple of minor problems connected with the first of these. In the first place, it is not clear from what source the author takes it, since the identical words are found in the Septuagint of 2 Samuel 22:3; Isaiah 8:17; 12:2. However, since the next quotation is from Isaiah 8:18, the presumption is that this is from Isaiah 8:17. The other problem is why the words are cited here (they say nothing about brothers). Perhaps it is because the context in Isaiah is full of the thought of the troubles that beset God's people, and our author may be thinking that these are good words to put before saints with problems: Jesus is brother to those who need Him. Or the thought may be that, as a man, Jesus trusted God just as we must do. In that case He shows that He is a brother by sharing our attitude.

In the last quotation believers are called "children," a word normally indicating little children. They are "given" by God whose supremacy is thus kept before us. It is not usual to have believers spoken of as Christ's children, though in John 21:5 He greets His followers with the same word as that used here (the NIV translates it there with "friends").

The three quotations indicate that Jesus shared the nature of His people and the thought is now developed further (vv. 14–15). The children have in common "flesh and blood," in which He also shared. That is to say, He lived the same kind of life as they did in the same kind of body. The purpose was that He might defeat the Devil. The Evil One is here described as "him who holds the power of death," but this must mean that his power operates only within the sphere of death—it is God who holds absolute power over death (Job 2:6; Luke 12:5), while Satan works only with the power that is permitted him. And that power is never for life but always for death. It was the work of the Devil that brought death into the world (Gen. 2:17; Rom. 5:12). The great thought our author brings out at this point is that the work of Christ means the destruction of the Devil's power and the gift of freedom to His people.

The atonement is many-sided (we have just seen that it is a process of bringing people to glory, v. 10, and of making them holy, v. 11). An important side is deliverance from the Devil and from the fear of death, a fear that was very real in the first century. The inscriptions on pagan tombs are eloquent of grief and hopelessness. Few things are more striking than the contrast between the richly ornamented expressions of despair on the tombs of pagans and the exuberant hope in the roughly scratched epitaphs in the catacombs where the Christians were buried. Christ did indeed free His people from the fear of death (cf. 1 Cor. 15:54–57). When the writer speaks of destroying Satan he does not, of course, mean that the Devil is slain or anything like that. He means that the power of the Evil One is nullified. The freedom Christ gives His people includes all the power they need to triumph over the Devil. They are no longer subject to him as they were before Christ saved them.

The verb translated "helps" (v. 16) means "takes hold of," usually with the idea of giving assistance, which is the justification of the translation of the NIV (cf. Luke 14:4). But it may be that the meaning here is not "helps" but "takes hold of," i.e., it was humanity He took to Himself (though, of course, with a view to helping it), not the nature of angels. And when one is a man he is not simply man in general, but a man of a particular human group. So our author particularizes with "Abraham's descendants" (cf. the description of Jesus as "the son of Abraham," Matt. 1:1).

The argument is taken a step further when we are informed that Jesus "had to" become like "his brothers." In order to bring about atonement for men, it was *necessary* that Jesus become a man like them. The Incarnation is the indispensable prelude to the Atonement. Any priest must be one with the people if he is to represent them. So Jesus became like us "in every way" (except, of course, in our sin, a point specifically mentioned a little later, 4:15). This becoming man had a definite purpose: "in order that he might become a merciful and faithful high priest. . . ." This is the first mention of Christ as a high priest in this epistle, a concept that means a great deal to the author and is peculiarly his own (no other New Testament writer speaks of Christ in this way). As happens with a number of his concepts, at this first introduction he simply mentions it. He will come back to it later and develop the thought, but here it is sufficient to introduce it. Sometimes he calls Jesus a priest and sometimes a high priest, but there seems no great difference, except that in some instances he is concerned with the Day of Atonement and then, of course, it is the high priest who is in view.

He characterizes the priest as both merciful and faithful. It is mercy that sinners need and this term is given some emphasis. But there are moral realities that cannot be overlooked and these are in mind in the adjective "faithful" and in the reminder that Christ's priestly service is service "to God" (who does not condone any sin). This point is further brought out in the rest of the verse, which should be taken in the sense of the NIV margin rather than the text. The verb has to do not with atonement in general, but with a specific aspect of the Atonement, namely the dealing with the wrath of God. All sin arouses that wrath (Rom. 1:18), and if we are to be saved it cannot be by ignoring the divine anger. It is part of the work of Jesus as our Great High Priest that He "makes propitiation," i.e., turns the wrath of God away from sinners. This is yet another facet of the Atonement and one we must not overlook: it was "the sins of the people" that aroused the wrath of God and as Christ puts those sins away He removes the divine wrath.

In the last verse of the chapter the writer goes on to the thought that the sufferings of Jesus enable Him to help us when we suffer. The specific suffering in mind is that which is bound up with temptation. Jesus had other sufferings (for example, on the cross, which is much in mind in this context). But here it is the suffering involved in temptation that is being considered. Temptation must have been an exceedingly painful experience for the spotless Son of God; it is part of life and He underwent it constantly. The temptation stories early in the synoptic Gospels bring this before the reader (Matt. 4:1–11; Mark 1:12; Luke 4:1–13), and we should not think that those temptations were an isolated experience. Luke explicitly says that the devil left Jesus "until an opportune time" (Luke 4:13), and in this epistle we read that Jesus was "tempted in every way, just as we are—yet was without sin" (4:15). Since He knows all that temptation involves He can help us. Notice the words "is able to help." Only the One who has been through temptation *can* help. When we are tempted we can confidently look to Him. He knows our weakness. He knows our need. He has Himself been where we are.

D. Superior to Moses (3:1–6)

The author concludes his demonstration of the greatness of Jesus by showing that He is superior to Moses. This seems to us an anticlimax, but we should bear in mind that Moses was put in a very high place by the Jews of that day. Moses had been the great leader who brought the people out of Egypt with the triumph at the Red Sea. It was under his leadership that the nation of Israel can be said to have emerged. He was the lawgiver, the man who wrote the words of the divine Law, the section of the Old Testament that the Jews regarded as the most significant part of their Bible. When God rebuked Aaron and Miriam for their presumption in placing themselves on a level with Moses, God said that He revealed Himself to prophets in visions and dreams but not so with Moses: "With him I speak face to face, clearly and not in riddles; he sees the form of the Lord" (Num. 12:8). When Moses came down from Mount Sinai with the tablets of the Law his face shone "because he had spoken with the Lord" and he had to put a veil over his face (Exod.34:29–35). There are rabbinic statements that say that Moses was greater than the angels. To show that Jesus was greater than Moses was thus to say something very important to first-century Jews. We should notice that in this comparison the writer does not belittle Moses in any way. He might well have drawn attention to occasions when Moses' conduct was less than ideal. But he does not. He is content to let the Jewish estimate of Moses stand and to show that, great as Moses was, Jesus is greater.

The writer greets his readers as "holy brothers" (a form of address found only here in the New Testament; but cf. Col. 1:2) and reminds them of their "heavenly calling" (v. 1). Thus he combines the notes of consecration ("holy"), affection ("brothers"), and relation to God ("calling"). He invites them to give serious attention to Jesus (notice the use of the human name) and speaks of Him as "apostle" and "high priest." "Apostle" means "someone who is sent"; the term is used of Jesus only here in the New Testament, but the thought that God "sent" Him is found frequently (John 3:17, etc.). The thought of mission is important. And Jesus' mission involved being "high priest," a thought that will be developed more fully later in the letter.

Two points that are singled out for contrast are faithfulness and honor. Moses had been faithful in God's house (Num. 12:7), which is high praise. But our author notices that Moses was faithful as a servant (v. 5): important though Moses was, he was essentially a subordinate. This is not belittling Moses but is a careful statement of exactly where he stood in God's household. However, Jesus' faithfulness was that of "a son over God's house" (v. 6). There is obviously a great difference between a son who is "over" the entire household and a man who may be excellent in the capacity of servant, but whose one function is to serve. The word for "servant" (v. 5) is found only here in the New Testament; it points to a servant in an honored place, but still a servant. The honored place is indicated by the addition "testifying to what would be said in the future": Moses gave important revelations and bore testimony to what would happen in days to come. Perhaps we should see something of Moses' greatness also in the twofold "all": he was faithful in "all" God's house and a servant in "all" God's house (vv. 2, 5). Other servants of God, like prophets, priests, or kings, had restricted spheres. Each was responsible for important work, but there was much that was beyond his scope. Moses had a responsibility in "all" the house.

Faithfulness is given the emphasis, but honor is also important. Here the writer sees Jesus as meriting greater honor "just as the builder of a house has greater honor than the house itself" (v. 3). The writer uses two Greek words, both of which the NIV renders "honor"; the first of these is more usually rendered "glory." Jesus is worthy of greater glory than Moses, just as a housebuilder merits greater honor than the house he builds, no matter how wonderful that house may be. No house originates itself. There must be a builder. The writer adds that "God is the builder of everything." There may be a hint here at the thought already expressed that God made everything through the Son (1:2). At any rate, the Son's activity as builder of the house rather than as a servant in it is stressed.

"House" is, of course, an ambiguous term. It can mean a physical building or it can be used in the sense of "household." The physical building may be in mind in some of the statements in this paragraph, but the idea of the household is certainly there and this is emphasized in the climax, "we are his house" (v. 6). The "house" is the people of God and there is some emphasis on "we." It is not the Jews who constitute the people of God, God's "house," but the Christians. Those who clung to Judaism over against Christianity were wrong on two counts: they preferred Moses the servant to Jesus the Son and they did not see that the Jews had forfeited their place as the people of God. Everything was new now that the Son had come.

There is a further point of some significance when the writer adds, "if we hold on to our courage and the hope of which we boast." The people of God are those who persevere. There will always be troubles and trials for the people of God. There will never be a time when courage and hope will not be needed. It is the mark of God's elect that they hold fast to these qualities. In the New Testament, "hope" may be used in much the same way as we use it, of a mild optimism about the future. But more characteristically it is used of the blazing certainty that the future will be well, despite the troubles it undoubtedly carries, for God is in it and we may rely on the promises of God.

Notice that the Savior is here called "Christ" for the first time in the epistle. The term lacks the article as it does also in 9:11, 24. It is found with the article ("the Christ") six times (3:14; 5:5; 6:1; 9:14, 28; 11:26), while "Jesus Christ" is found three times (10:10; 13:8, 21). The term, of course, means "anointed" or "Messiah." We have already seen that this author uses the name Jesus nine times. Both the human nature and the messiahship matter to him.

For Further Study

1. Look up "angel" in a Bible dictionary or encyclopedia. What does Hebrews 1 teach about angels?
2. Make a list of all the ways in which the author shows the superiority of Jesus Christ.
3. What is the importance of the real humanity of Jesus?
4. In what ways does the author show that Jesus is greater than Moses? What is the importance of this?
5. What does this passage say to people today who see Jesus as simply a great religious teacher?

Chapter 3

The Promised Rest

(Hebrews 3:7–4:13)

Our author has made it clear that Jesus is a great Savior. He ends his treatment of that subject by showing that He is infinitely superior to Moses, whom the Jews revered highly. Now he moves on to the consequences for the lives of God's servants. He sees the Christian way as better than the way of Judaism, and he brings out his point by a consideration of the "rest" that the Israelites did not enter (Ps. 95:11), but which is open for the followers of Christ.

A. Scriptural Basis (3:7–11)

He begins with a quotation from Psalm 95, which he introduces with the words, "So, as the Holy Spirit says." The writer is fond of ascribing the words of Scripture to the divine Author. In chapter 1 he has a string of quotations introduced by "to which of the angels did God ever say . . . ?" (1:5), and in 2:12 it is Jesus who speaks the words of Psalm 22:22. Now it is the Spirit (cf. 9:8; 10:15; Acts 28:25). It is very important for this author that the words of Scripture are the words of God. He starts his quotation with the word "today," a word he uses eight times in all. By having this word first he gives it emphasis. It is important to hear the voice of God and act on it *now*. There is a note of urgency. Obedience must not be deferred.

The quotation from Psalm 95:7–11 deals with a situation in which the Israelites disobeyed God in the wilderness. Their persistent disobedience caused God to swear that they would never enter His rest. The incident primarily in mind is the occasion when there was no water and Israel put God to the test (Exod. 17:1–7); the narrative ends with the words, "he called the place Massah and Meribah because the Israelites quarreled and because they tested the Lord. . . ." In the psalm, the NIV has "Meribah" and "Massah," but here, "rebellion" and "testing" (v. 8). The reason is that our author quotes from the Septuagint, where these names are always translated by terms like "rebellion" and "testing."

The writer calls on his readers to listen to the voice of God and not to harden their hearts, i.e., not to walk determinedly in their own ways, rejecting what God has said to them. This the Israelites did constantly. For forty years they saw the mighty works of God (v. 9), but instead of reacting with awe and gratitude they kept testing God (the word "tested" in v. 9 can also be translated "tempted"), and trying Him out (perhaps the thought is that they wanted to see how far they could go). Sinful men persistently rejected humble obedience.

The result was that God was "angry with that generation" (v. 10). The wrath of God is an important topic in both the Old Testament and the New. It stands for the settled opposition of God's holy nature to everything that is evil. Perhaps "wrath" and "anger" are not ideal words, because as we use them they often include elements of lack of self-control and the like, which we do not attribute to God. But we have no better words to express the truth that God is implacably opposed to all evil. Scripture is clear about the fact and these are the terms it uses. So here, faced with sin, God did not say, "It does not matter." It did matter. God was angry. And angry with them all, for "generation" here denotes all the Israelites of that time. There are two counts against them, the first being "their hearts are always going astray" (v. 10). "Hearts" stands for the whole of man's inner state and includes thoughts and will as well as emotions. In their innermost being the Israelites went astray. It could not be said that their sinning was just on the surface and that at heart they were all right. They did wrong by virtue of character, because of what they were like deep down. And they did it "always"—their going astray was no occasional accident.

The second count is their ignorance: "they have not known my ways." Sometimes ignorance is innocent: people do not always have the opportunity or the capacity for knowledge. But ignorance can be blameworthy. When a man can well know something and simply refuses to take the opportunity, he is responsible. That is the way it was in the wilderness. What God did throughout the forty years was before the people's eyes, but they still did not know His ways. That could arise only from spiritual neglect.

The result was God's anger and His oath: they would never enter His rest (v. 11). The oath is the most solemn form of assertion and it shows the seriousness with which God took the rebellious spirit of the Israelites. We read of this oath at the time the spies returned from their survey of the Promised Land (Num. 14:21–23). They had seen the land God had for them and recognized it as a goodly land (Num. 13:27). But they did not believe that God could give it to them; the difficulties were too many (Num. 13:31–33). So they cut themselves off from the blessing and God swore that they would never enter into it. "Rest" indicates the end of hard work, repose in the blessing of God.

B. Some Did Not Enter the Rest (3:12–19)

Psalm 95 makes it clear both that God has a rest for His people and that the wilderness generation did not enter the rest that was set before them. This is a message of hope, but also a warning to the readers of the epistle. There is a rest set before them, but the fate of the wilderness generation shows that they will not automatically enter the blessing. It is possible for them to reject it and lose their opportunity. So the writer urges his readers to see to it that none has "a sinful, unbelieving heart" (v. 12). He has spoken of Jesus as "faithful" and added that Moses was faithful also (v. 2), so they have good examples. To be "unbelieving" is the opposite, while "heart" points to the inner being, to unbelief at the core. This means turning away from God, where "turns away" is a strong expression that should rather be "rebels against." To rebel against "the living God" (cf. 9:14; 10:31; 12:22) is the height of folly as well as the depth of sin. In one sense, to go back from Christianity to Judaism is still to serve the same God. But the writer sees this as being really an act of rebellion, for it means the rejection of the supreme revelation that God has made in Jesus.

But he looks to his readers to encourage and help one another (cf. Matt. 18:15–17), rather than to rebel. "Daily" is important—encouragement should be constant, while "as long as it is called Today" reminds us that present opportunity does not last forever. It should be taken while it is here and used to see that not one member of the fellowship is harmed. It is possible for people to be "hardened," which points to a concentration on their own welfare and a lack of compassion for others; it is not a mark of enlightened self-interest, but the result of "sin's deceitfulness." In the context it seems clear that the readers were feeling the temptation to leave the Christian way and to go back to Judaism. This would immediately release them from the persecution that always threatened the Christians (cf. 1 Peter 4:12–16) and give them the safety that resulted from being recognized members of a permitted religion. But to see the situation in this way is to take a superficial view. The purchase of freedom from persecution at the cost of losing Christ means the payment of a huge and tragic price. It is to lose eternal salvation in order to gain what can never be more than a temporary advantage.

This leads to the thought of perseverance. The writer has already stressed its importance (v. 6) and he will come back to it (10:26). His warning here is not unlike the warning Jesus gave in His interpretation of the parable of the Sower: "Others, like seed sown on rocky places, hear the word and at once receive it with joy. But since they have no root, they last only a short time. When trouble or persecution comes because of the word, they quickly fall away" (Mark 4:16–17). It is possible to feel a superficial attraction to Christianity, to appreciate the warmth of Christian fellowship, or to be attracted by the wonder of the love of God in sending His Son to die for our salvation. But if there is no genuine conversion, no real commitment of the whole person (Matt. 22:37), there is no real partaking of Christ and thus no perseverance. Where people really share in Christ they "hold firmly till the end"; conversely, when they hold on to the end, this is evidence that they have come to share in Christ. Notice the paradox: "We have come to share in Christ" points to the divine gift, while "if we hold firmly" indicates human effort. Our perseverance is due to the grace of God and we must never regard it as something we achieve by our own effort. But it is also true that we must not regard our effort as unimportant. We are to be active, not passive, as we seek to live out our faith. The readers can remember the "confidence" they had at the beginning of their Christian experience. The memory should spur them to keep it to the end.

The writer goes on to quote Psalm 95:7–8 a second time to reinforce his point. The Israelites in the wilderness had hardened their hearts—the very opposite of the attitude he looks for in his readers. He goes on to emphasize the point with a series of rhetorical questions. He asks first "Who were they who heard and rebelled?" When the people heard the voice of God they might have been expected to obey. Instead they "rebelled"; the writer uses a striking expression (found only here in the New Testament), which connotes bitterness. The Israelites in the wilderness should have been full of gratitude to God for His deliverance of the nation from Egypt; instead they were embittered and rebellious when they met the hardships that were a necessary part of being free.

The writer answers his question by asking a second question: "Were they not all those Moses led out of Egypt?" It is true that there was the tiniest of tiny remnants that remained faithful, for Joshua and Caleb did not go along with the rebellious. But that does not invalidate the argument. It was the nation as a whole, "all" those who came out of Egypt, who were embittered and rebellious. The readers should not be complacent. A whole generation who had seen the wonderful works of God had yet become rebels.

Again the writer asks a question and answers it with another question (v. 17). He spoke earlier of the forty years in the wilderness (v. 9), but there he was concerned with the fact that all during this long period the people had seen God's works and had "tried" Him. Now his point is rather that throughout that period of time the wrath of God was exercised toward the rebels. In his answering question he uses an emphatic form (which he employs elsewhere only in 1:14); it indicates the certainty of the conclusion to be drawn, a certainty the NEB brings out by translating, "With those, surely, who had sinned." There was not the slightest doubt about it. It was the sinners in the wilderness against whom God's anger burned: their "bodies fell in the desert." The writer uses words reminiscent of Numbers 14:29: "In this desert your bodies will fall" (cf. Num.

14:32). It had been prophesied that those who disobeyed God would be destroyed in the desert. And they were destroyed there.

In making his third point, our author embodies his answer in his question instead of making it a second question. He refers to the oath God swore (cf. v. 11), which brings him back to the thought of rest. Because they disobeyed they forfeited the blessing of rest that would otherwise have been theirs. There is a question as to whether we should understand the last word of verse 18 in the sense of "disobeyed" or "disbelieved" (NIV mg.). It is likely that we should take it in the sense of the text, but "disbelieved" is not far away, as we see from the following verse. The conclusion of this part of the argument is that it was unbelief that prevented them from entering the promised rest. The writer does not see God as an arbitrary despot cutting the Israelites off from blessing—they cut themselves off. Their unbelief made it impossible ("they were not able") for them to enter. The "rest" of which our author is writing is a rest that involves a right spiritual attitude: God says it is "my rest" (v. 11). If this attitude is replaced with unbelief, then there is no question of their entering. Unbelief simply *cannot* rest in the Lord.

C. Christians Enter the Rest (4:1–10)

It is unthinkable to our author that any promise of God should fail of fulfillment. God has promised a rest for those who are His; therefore the people of God will enter that rest. It is, of course, possible that some people will cut themselves off from that rest, but that does not alter the basic truth. There will be a rest and God will bring His people into it. In the preceding section it has been made clear that Israel of old failed to enter God's rest. So entrance into the rest is open, but no one has entered. What follows? Some one else will enter: the persevering, believing people of God. The readers should not throw away the blessing that is held before them. There is nothing automatic about their entering it. Israel had thrown away its opportunity. Let not those who have professed to be Christ's make the same mistake.

The writer makes it clear that "the promise of entering his rest still stands" (v. 1). The idea of promise, especially of any promise God makes, means a great deal to him and he comes back to it often (he uses the word "promise" fourteen times, more than it is used in any other New Testament book). God has promised that some will enter His rest, and God's promise will certainly be fulfilled. He urges his readers to fear lest they miss it. "Let us be careful" (NIV) is not strong enough; the verb means "to fear" and comes first in the Greek sentence, which gives it emphasis. There are some things of which God's people do well to be afraid, and the fear of turning from God is one to which our author returns (e.g., 10:27, 31). There is a fear of God that is right and proper (12:28–29), and when people have this fear they need have no other fear. In fact, they have confidence (13:6). All this gives support to such a rendering of the following words as "none of you must think that he has come too late for it" (JB). Taken in this way, the words would be an encouragement to timid believers who thought they might miss God's rest.

However, the context favors the view that we have here a warning rather than an encouragement. The verb the JB translates as "think" is taken by most translators and commentators in the sense of "seem," "be ajudged," or "be found" (NIV). The writer warns his readers against falling short, and by putting it gently like this he is simply uttering a warning, not saying that some of them will actually miss the rest. He wants them to take their situation seriously. Ancient Israel had had great opportunities and had missed out. Let the readers not make the same mistake.

Both Israel and the readers had received good news from God. The verb *euangelizomai* (from which we get "evangelize") means "to bring good news" generally, but in the Christian sense is used of the good news of what God has done for us in sending His Son to die for our salvation. It can thus mean "to preach the gospel," which is the sense the NIV takes here. Others understand it more generally, as does the RSV: "good news came to us just as to them." If we understand that God's message to Israel of old was "the gospel," we will accept the meaning of the NIV; if we think it was more general we will follow the RSV. What is beyond doubt is that words from God came to both—in this respect there is no difference between them.

This carries a warning, because "the message they heard was of no value to them," a truth the writer has been emphasizing. The manuscripts give us different readings here and the scholars are not unanimous as to which we should accept. Basically there are two possibilities, one of which the NIV has put in the text, the other in the margin. If we accept the text, the meaning is that they did not really believe the words they heard (did not combine the message with faith); if we prefer the margin, the writer is saying that they did not share in the faith of people like Joshua and Caleb who heard the same message and believed. Whichever reading we accept, the writer is saying in the end that the Israelites of old failed to profit from the message because they did not believe. There is no substitute for faith.

Faith is a topic of great importance in this epistle. Chapter 11 contains the most sustained treatment of faith in the New Testament. The author uses the word thirty-two times, which is the most it is used in any New Testament writing except Romans (which has it forty times). Faith may mean trust in God or trust in Christ; in this epistle it is often the former. But for our author there is no real difference. How could anyone really trust God without trusting Christ? That is his objection to Judaism. Jewish people said that they believed in God but they rejected Jesus, God's supreme revelation. This is for him a complete impossibility. The same God spoke both through the Old Testament and through His Son (cf. 1:1–2).

It is Christians ("we who have believed") who "enter that rest." Once again we have the importance of faith. Unbelief and disobedience shut people out from God's rest. The writer lets his readers be in no doubt about this. He has a somewhat complicated argument (vv. 3–5). He says that, after completing the work of creation, "on the seventh day God rested from all his work." The people of God are invited to share in God's rest, which clearly means very great blessing. But there were some, the wilderness generation, whose conduct and attitude were such that God swore that they would never enter the promised rest. The writer has already quoted Psalm 95:7–11 and Psalm 95:7–8 (3:7–11, 15) and now he twice quotes verse 11 of the same psalm. This psalm is important and it says something significant about the ultimate blessing of the people of God. The oath of God is impressive. It indicates that, while God opens up the way into rich blessing for His people, He is equally determined that those who walk in the paths of unbelief and disobedience will forever be cut off from that blessing.

Some have thought that entering the rest meant entering the Promised Land, Canaan. But this does not satisfy our author and he goes on to make this clear. Perhaps the opening words of verse 6 would be better rendered, "Since therefore it remains . . ." (RSV; cf. KJV). The line of thought is that God has determined that people will share with Him in the blessings of rest. The preceding paragraph has made it plain that the people of old did not secure that blessing. Therefore the position remains open, so to speak. There must be someone to enter the rest, for God's promise cannot fail. Since those who might have been expected to enter it had failed, God must be preparing someone else. As in verse 2, the author speaks of the wilderness generation as the recipients of the gospel or good news, and as in 3:18, he assigns their failure to secure the blessing to their disobedience. The point he makes is important and he does not hesitate to repeat his arguments. The readers must be brought to see that disobedience to God's word is a very serious matter. It had excluded a whole generation from entering rest. He might have gone on to show that it had excluded later generations also, but he prefers to stick to what the psalm says about one particular group of Israelites. What the Bible says about this group is plain, but it needed to be pointed out. Among the Jews it was held that somehow the wilderness generation would be included in the number of the saved. A fervent nationalism insisted that all Jews would come under the saving activity of their God, and while some specially hardened sinners would no doubt be excluded, a whole generation would not; God did not lack the means to bring those sinners in the wilderness into the number of His saved ones. When our author insists that their disobedience had cut them off from God's salvation he is contradicting a firmly held Jewish opinion.

He proceeds to show the importance of the word "Today." Psalm 95 was written centuries after the wilderness period. It was written by David, though we should notice the writer's characteristic way of putting it: it was God who spoke, and He did so "through David." When David wrote, the wilderness generation had long since perished but God still said "Today." God still held out the promise of rest to those who "hear his voice" and "do not harden [their] hearts." Clearly the psalm had something to say to the readers of this epistle.

This is further explained in verse 8. Some might think that God's rest meant rest in the land of Canaan, when Israel's enemies had been defeated and the land was their secure possession. This was the achievement of Joshua. But the psalm with its "Today" came much later than Joshua. If physical Canaan had been in mind, "God would not have spoken later about another day." The date of the psalm is thus important and so, probably, is the name of the leader. "Joshua" is the way we render in English the Hebrew name of the leader who followed Moses. But the Greek form of that name is the name we put into English as "Jesus," and it is "Jesus" that we find in the epistle at this point (cf. KJV). The NIV's "Joshua" is surely correct, because it leaves us in no doubt as to the identity of the man who is meant. But the Greek-speaking original readers of this letter would see in "Jesus" a reminder that their Leader and Savior was calling them on into rest (cf. Matt. 11:28–30). The first "Jesus" had not brought his people into rest. The second "Jesus" would. Let the readers beware of missing out.

But Joshua had not brought the people into that rest, since the psalm spoke of it as open some hundreds of years after Joshua; the "Sabbath-rest" therefore still remains. Here our author uses an unusual word, one of which we have no recorded examples before this passage and which the writer appears to have manufactured himself. It is correctly formed on the word for "Sabbath" and there is no doubt about its meaning. But nobody seems to have had his idea of "rest" previously, and he uses here an unusual word to match his unusual idea. The Old Testament spoke of rest on the Sabbath (Exod. 16:23, etc.) and of a certain rest in the land (Josh. 23:1). There was a domestic rest (Ruth 1:9), and Job looked longingly at the rest in death (Job 3:17). There are other forms of rest, some of which have a markedly spiritual tone (e.g., Isa. 30:15; Jer. 6:16), but none that matches the "rest" set forth in this passage.

Some students understand verse 10 to refer to Christ, who has completed His work of salvation and thus has entered God's rest. But the verse rather appears to be of general application: the writer is referring to any of God's people. There is a further problem, namely, as to whether the writer is referring to a present or a future rest. Despite the urgings of some scholars who argue strongly for one or the other, we should probably understand it in both senses. It is true of the here and now, for those who put their trust in Christ and His finished work do indeed rest from their own work. For them there is no striving to achieve salvation through their own efforts but a quiet resting in what God has done for them. And it is true of the future, for in the world to come those who are in Christ enter a rest from this world's strivings, a rest from all their work. In both cases it can be said that we rest from our work "just as God did from his."

D. Exhortation to Enter the Rest (4:11–13)

The writer rounds off his treatment of this unusual and interesting aspect of the Christian salvation with an urgent invitation to his readers to make that rest their own. He does not adopt a position of superiority but includes himself in the exhortation, "Let *us*. . . ." There is something paradoxical about making every effort to enter rest, but the meaning is not that we should work hard at resting. Rather, the thrust of the words is that we are to take the thought of God's rest with the utmost seriousness. It is important, and it is important that we enter it. This demands from us more than an occasional fleeting thought. It means that we should concentrate on making it our own.

The writer has been concerned about disobedience before (3:18; 4:6) and he comes back to it once more. He is clear that the way had been open to people in earlier days but that they had disobeyed God and had cut themselves off from the blessing. He does not wish to see his readers following the same path, so he continues to warn them against disobedience. They had had an "example," not only of disobedience, but of the consequences that inevitably follow.

He brings this out by referring to "the word of God," which means anything that God says, particularly the words spoken through the prophets and other writers of Old Testament books, and most of all what God said to men in Jesus Christ. The author began the letter by pointing to the revelation in Christ as the supreme revelation and this thought is before him constantly. John, of course, refers to Jesus as "the Word" (John 1:1), but that is not what is meant here. Rather, it is everything that God says. This word of God is seen as vital and active. In the Greek, "living" comes first in the clause and is separated from "active," which gives it strong emphasis: "For *living* is the word of God and active." We are not to think of dead words in a book, a kind of parchment pope. We are to think rather of any utterance of God as full of vital force, as dynamic, as active in bringing about God's purpose (cf. Isa. 55:10–11).

God's word is then compared to a sword. The point here is its capacity to penetrate. A "double-edged" sword had great cutting power and the word of God is sharper than any such sword. The sword penetrates physical matter, but the word of God penetrates the innermost parts of man.

The writer does not mean that this word actually divides the soul from the spirit or that it literally splits one's joints from the marrow. He is saying that no part of us is immune to the effects of God's word. It penetrates our deepest recesses.

More, it judges us. It judges even "the thoughts and attitudes of the heart," those deep and hidden parts of life we feel to be our very own. No one can know our secret thoughts, our hidden attitudes. No one, says our author, but God. God's word knows what is going on deep down in us and that word judges us. We cannot assume that we can get away with things before God in the way we can get away with them before other people. God knows.

"Nothing in all creation is hidden from God's sight" (v. 13). That is logical enough, for it is God who made all that is. And if He knows everything about all creation, it is obviously quite useless to think that we can keep anything back from Him. Before Him "Everything is uncovered," "uncovered" literally meaning "naked." It is used of a body without clothing (Acts 19:16) or of the soul without the body (2 Cor. 5:3), and of other forms of "nakedness"; there is no covering that will shield us from the living word of God. The writer adds a vivid word that we translate as "laid bare." It is a verb from the same stem as "neck" and was used by wrestlers. They had evidently discovered a hold that involved the neck in some way and that was so powerful that when it was secured victory was certain. Unfortunately, this does not seem to suit the context here, though there are some who take the words to mean: "All things are naked and prostrate before his eyes." Others have thought it means "expose the neck" or the like. This would not fit the wrestlers very well, so it has been suggested that we should think rather of sacrificial victims. The head would be bent back to expose the throat so that the animal could be killed more easily. Unfortunately there are no examples known of such a use. One early Father, Chrysostom, held that the term referred to the skinning of animals so that their inward parts were exposed. This may be right, but the reference is not obvious. In the end we must be content with saying that the writer has clearly used a picturesque word, one that gives emphasis to the idea of exposure, but whose exact meaning is no longer open to us.

There is a lesser problem about the concluding words of the verse. They possibly mean "him with whom we have to do" (KJV, RSV). But the NIV seems more likely to be correct: "him to whom we must give account"; the expression is one used by accountants. Thus the final reason the author gives for our pressing on to enter the rest is that we are accountable to God, the God before whom all things, even the most secret things, are open and exposed.

For Further Study

1. What does "Sabbath-rest" mean for the Christian?
2. How does the writer bring out the seriousness of disobedience?
3. Notice the ways the quotations from Scripture are introduced. What do they tell us about the authorship of Scripture?

Chapter 4

A Great High Priest

(Hebrews 4:14–5:11)

It is only in this epistle that we find Jesus described as a priest or high priest. The writer has already introduced this thought (2:17; 3:1) and he now proceeds to develop the theme. It is an enlightening way of looking at who Jesus is and what He has done in bringing us salvation, and all subsequent generations of believers have been indebted to our author.

A. Our Confidence (4:14–16)

The first point is that, because of who and what our High Priest is, we can have confidence in our approach to God. "Therefore" ties this part of the argument to the preceding. The writer is embarking on a new aspect of his argument, but it is not unconnected with what he has just said: because of the fullness of meaning of the rest into which God's people enter, certain things follow. Interestingly, the writer begins by speaking of Jesus as having "gone through the heavens." He sometimes thinks of heaven as a unity and simply says "heaven" (e.g., 9:24; 11:12). But the Jews often thought of diversity in heaven, and in writings like the Talmud we find references to seven heavens; Paul could refer to "the third heaven" (2 Cor. 12:2). Our author does not commit himself to any particular view but says that Jesus has passed through whatever heavens there are. This is a way of saying that He is in the very presence of God, not in some inferior part of heaven. He speaks of the Savior with the human name "Jesus" and immediately adds "the Son of God," which brings out His greatness. The writer likes to think of Jesus as God's Son (as in his opening words, 1:1–2), though he does not use this exact expression very often (see 6:6; 7:3; 10:29). Both aspects are important in a priest: he must be one with those he represents and must also have access to God. The fact that we have such a High Priest is the basis of an exhortation, "let us hold firmly to the faith we profess." Clearly the writer is concerned lest his readers slip away from the faith, and he loses no opportunity of reminding them of the importance of standing fast.

He proceeds to emphasize the importance of Jesus' real humanity. He has done this before, when bringing out the point that Jesus died for everyone, for which purpose He "was made a little lower than the angels" (2:9). Now the thought is rather that as a high priest He is perfectly one with us in our weakness. He does not merely contemplate our weakness from a safe distance. He knows what it is like, for He came where we are and underwent temptation just as we do. The writer has already pointed out that this involved suffering on His part and that because of this He is able to help those who are tempted (2:18). Now he adds the point that Jesus' temptations were like ours—"in every way" stresses the likeness. Sinners can never say, "It was easier for Him." It was not. He experienced all the temptations common to man. In fact, His temptations were greater than ours because He did not yield. The only person who knows the full force of a given temptation is the one who resists it right to the end. The one who gives in at some point along the way does not know the fierceness of the temptation that would follow at a later point. But Jesus did not give in. He knows all the power and all the force of temptation, not only the small part that sinners who give way know.

There is one possible exception. The words at the end of verse 15 mean literally "apart from sin," and they have been taken to mean that there was one temptation He did not experience, the temptation that arises out of a sin previously committed. We are more ready to commit a sin we have previously committed than a totally new one. But "yet was without sin" (NIV) has the support of many scholars. It is unlikely that the writer is trying to differentiate between the temptation of a sin previously committed and that of "new" sin. He is simply stating firmly that Jesus did not sin at all. It is important that our High Priest was completely victorious over sin.

This is the basis for an appeal to "approach the throne of grace with confidence." This is the only place in the Bible where we read of "the throne of grace," though there are similar expressions, like "throne of glory" (Jer. 14:21; 17:12). Among the Jews it was sometimes held that God sat on "the throne of judgment" when He was punishing people and on "the throne of mercy" when He was forgiving them. The meaning here is obviously that God is a gracious God and that when He sits on His throne in majesty it is so that He may dispense grace. Indeed, the writer goes on to speak of receiving mercy and finding grace when these are needed.

We should not overlook the force of "Let us approach. . . ." In all the religious systems of antiquity the worshipers approached their god through the ministry of an earthly priest or high priest. But because of what Christ has done Christians approach God directly. They need no other mediator (cf. 8:6; 1 Tim. 2:5). And they approach "with confidence." They need not come hesitantly as those unsure of the reception they will receive. Because of who their High Priest is and His intimate knowledge of their needs and their temptations there is no place for doubts. The way to the throne is open, the throne that is "the throne of grace," and the worshiper may know that mercy and grace are to be found there. Well may the believer come in confidence.

B. The Qualities Required in High Priests (5:1–4)

Everyone in antiquity knew what a high priest was and what sort of person was needed for such an office. So the writer reminds his readers that a high priest is "selected" (perhaps better, "taken"; he is not simply chosen, but taken from the very community he is to represent) "from among men." A high priest must not be imposed from without. He belongs to the community on whose behalf he is to minister.

Although he belongs to the community, his ministry is concerned with "matters related to God." The earthly and the heavenly aspects of his calling both have their place. The particular matter related to God the writer picks out is that of offering "gifts and sacrifices for sins." A high priest may do other things, but it is this offering of sacrifice that is central. Some differentiate between the "gifts," taken to be the offerings of cereals and the like, and the "sacrifices," which are seen as the offering of animals. But the writer does not seem to be making such a distinction. He is affirming that the duty of the high priest is to engage in the offering of sacrifice with a view to putting away the sins of the worshipers.

This requires from the priest a right attitude toward the worshipers. He must be able "to deal gently" with the people. This unusual verb (found only here in the New Testament) denotes the taking of a moderate line. The Stoics sought after the ideal of being quite free from emotion; by contrast, this verb was used in Greek philosophy to denote "the well-regulated restraint of emotion" (Héring). Here it refers to the exercise of compassion. A godly high priest might be tempted to feel anger and exasperation at the sins of the people, but he cannot well represent them in a mood like that. Rather, he should take the middle course, reprobating the sin indeed, but being compassionate to the sinner. He will realize that some sin is due to ignorance (would people commit a sin if they really understood all that it meant?), some also to error. He will realize, too, that he himself "is subject to weakness." Such considerations mean that a true high priest will "deal gently" with the people while at the same time refusing to condone their sin.

Because of his personal moral frailty the high priest must offer sacrifices for his own sins as well as for those of the people he represents. Indeed, in the sacrificial system of Israel he had to offer himself first, for only when his own sin had been dealt with was he in a position to minister on behalf of others. For example, on the Day of Atonement he had to offer a bull "for his own sin offering to make atonement for himself and his household" before he proceeded to make atonement for the people (Lev. 16:3,

6, 11). Sin is serious and the high priest understands that his own sin is as serious as any, perhaps even more so; only after it has been dealt with can he minister on behalf of others.

To minister on behalf of others as high priest was such a great honor that no one might presume to take it upon himself. One could be high priest only if God called him to the task. This had happened with Aaron (Exod. 28:1–3), with his son Eleazar (Num. 20:25–26), and with their successors (Num. 25:10–13). No personal call is recorded of later individuals, but it is clear that they exercised their function only because God had chosen the line of Aaron. When anyone outside that line presumed to act as a priest he was rejected and punished, as in the cases of Korah (Num. 16), Saul (1 Sam. 13:8–14), and Uzziah (2 Chron. 26:16–21).

In summary, a high priest must be taken from among those he represents, and he must have a proper sympathy with them. He must understand their limitations and indeed experience them himself. And only one who is called by God is qualified to fill the role of high priest.

C. Christ's Qualifications as High Priest (5:5–11)

Now that we have seen what is required in a high priest we are in a position to see that Jesus perfectly fulfilled these requirements. The writer reverses the order he has just laid down and deals with the divine call first, then goes on to the human weakness. He began his argument that Christ is greater than any angel by quoting Psalm 2:7 (see 1:5), and he does so again. The point now is that this psalm makes clear the thought of a divine call, a call to fulfill all that is involved in being the Son of God, which, of course, is infinitely greater than being a high priest and includes all that is in the lesser office. That this is recorded in Scripture makes it quite plain that Christ "did not take upon himself" the honor. It was given Him by God.

A second quotation applies specifically to the priesthood, for in another place (Ps. 110:4) God says, "You are a priest forever, in the order of Melchizedek." This is our author's first use of the word "priest," a term he will use fourteen times in all, though it is used no more than five times in any other New Testament book. No one else makes such use of the idea of priesthood. He uses it in a variety of ways, sometimes to refer to priests in general (e.g., 7:14), sometimes with reference to the Levitical priests (7:20, etc.). In chapter 7 he uses it of Melchizedek and there are important passages in which he uses it of Christ (5:6; 7:11, 15, 17, 21; 10:21). As we have already noticed, there seems little difference between calling Christ "priest" and "high priest." The essential thing about a priest is his offering of sacrifice (10:11, and for the high priest, 5:1; 8:3); this way of looking at Christ brings out the fact that His essential work for us is that of offering the one sacrifice that can take away sins. The author has put us greatly in his debt by his unusual and effective handling of this imagery.

As he has done with other concepts, the writer simply introduces the concept of the priesthood like that of Melchizedek and leaves it. He will come back to it later (in chap. 7) and develop the thought. Most translations refer to "the order" of Melchizedek, which is not quite what the writer is saying. There was no "order" of this sort, no series of priests stemming from Melchizedek—he was unique. What the writer is saying is that Christ's priesthood was like that of Melchizedek rather than like that of Aaron. The particular feature he selects for mention is that Melchizedek's priesthood is "forever"; it does not end and this is the wonderful thing about the priesthood of Christ.

Now he turns to the other characteristic of priesthood and goes on to show that Christ is one with us because He shares our weakness. The NIV renders "during the days of Jesus' life on earth" (v. 7), which gives the correct sense but scarcely brings out the force of the word "flesh": "during the days of His flesh." This term has associations of physical weakness and is probably used for that reason. The following words are quite general and might apply to a number of situations, but most agree that Gethsemane is particularly in mind. None of our accounts of what happened in the Garden tell us of "loud cries and tears," so the writer had access to information not recorded in our Gospels. The reference to "the one who could save him from death" certainly looks like a reference to Jesus' prayer in the Garden as He faced death.

Commentators differ in their understanding of the words "and he was heard because of his reverent submission." Many agree that any prayer of Jesus will necessarily have been answered and that this is the meaning of "was heard" here. But Jesus was not saved from death. He died. How then was His prayer "heard"? One explanation is that the word translated "reverent submission" can mean "godly fear" and that we might take the meaning here to be, "he was saved from being afraid of death." Another is that Jesus prayed, not to be delivered from death, but to be delivered from dying in the Garden. A third suggests that we should think of His prayer as being that He would be delivered out of the state of death (i.e., after He had died), not that He should be delivered from dying. Such explanations are ingenious, but they do not do justice to the language used. Rather, we should bear in mind that Jesus' prayer was, "Father, if you are willing, take this cup from me; yet not my will, but yours be done" (Luke 22:42). Jesus did not pray simply that He would not die, but that the will of the Father be done. His prayer was answered in that that will was done, and in the process Jesus was given the strength to go through all the horror that dying for sinners means. We should not think this strange. Answered prayer not uncommonly means that the intention of the prayer is fulfilled, but not in the precise terms that the praying person expects.

Continuing the theme of the oneness of Christ with His people, the writer points out that, Son though He was, "he learned obedience from what he suffered" (5:8). The thought that Jesus "learned obedience" is unexpected but points to an important truth. It is one thing to say (and firmly believe) that I am ready to obey even though it should mean suffering and another thing actually to obey and undergo the suffering. Jesus was always ready to obey (we must not think that the writer means that He passed from a state of disobedience to one of obedience—that is unthinkable). But in His earthly life He was not only ready to obey, He actually did obey and suffered in the process.

A similar remark must be made about the further thought that He was "made perfect." The writer does not mean that there was a time when Jesus was imperfect and that He went on to become perfect. There are different kinds of perfection. The perfection of the bud is one thing and the perfection of the flower another. Jesus always had the perfection of being ready to suffer, but He added to that the perfection of having actually suffered (cf. 2:10).

It was through this perfection of suffering that Jesus "became the source of eternal salvation for all who obey him" (v. 9). There was a cost in bringing about our salvation and Jesus paid the price. The expression "eternal salvation" is found only here in the New Testament; it is much more usual to find references to "eternal life." It reminds us that the salvation Christ brings reaches as far as salvation can. The addition "for all who obey him" does not mean that they merit their salvation by their obedience. Rather, they are those who have been obedient to the call to trust Christ for salvation and who live out what it means to be saved by being obedient in daily life (cf. comments on 3:14).

The writer has now shown that the two qualifications he has listed are to be found in Jesus: He was called by God and He is one of us, knowing our weaknesses and limitations. So the author goes on to say that He "was designated by God to be high priest." The writer will speak of Jesus as high priest often throughout this epistle, but he makes it clear that this is not his idea. It was God who made Christ high priest. As in verse 6, this is a priesthood like that of Melchizedek. What this means remains to be developed, but it is significant enough for the writer to insist on it already here. Many (including the NIV) take verse 11 as the beginning of a new paragraph, but it seems likely that we should take it as the ending of the previous paragraph. The writer has much to say about the subject of Melchizedek and he will come back to it in chapter 7. But he defers it a little and reminds his readers that they are "slow to learn." Several times he makes it clear that he expected from them a better understanding of the Christian way than they in fact have, and that applies also to this subject. Perhaps we should notice that the NIV's "you are" is more literally "you have become"; the writer is not referring to natural endowment but to an acquired state.

For Further Study

1. Look up "priest" and "high priest" in a Bible dictionary or encyclopedia. Essentially, what did a priest do? How does knowledge of the functions of priest and high priest help us understand the passage?
2. Gather the passages that tell us of Jesus' weakness and the like. What do they tell us of His real humanity?
3. In what ways did God call His high priests?

Chapter 5

The Danger of Apostasy

(Hebrews 5:12–6:20)

That Christ is to be seen as a priest like Melchizedek brings us to the thought that the readers will find this hard to understand because they have not made the progress in the faith that they should have, and this leads to the warning that they must beware lest they slip out of Christian things altogether. It is important that they take stock of themselves and realize something of the real riches in Christ that they were in danger of losing for some illusory worldly gain.

A. Failure to Progress in the Faith (5:12–14)

The first point the writer makes here is that the readers have been Christians for some time and that they ought by now to be teachers (v. 12). Instead, they are lacking in the understanding of even the most basic things about Christianity. "The elementary truths" translates an expression with a meaning like "the ABC." It does not mean even a moderate advance but the first and basic teachings. It is devastating to apply such an expression to people who by rights should have been teachers. They must go right back to first principles. "God's word" is more literally "the oracles of God" (KJV), which may mean that which is written in the Old Testament (the same expression is used in Rom. 3:2; cf. Acts 7:38). That is certainly the main thrust, though we should bear in mind that the expression is general enough to cover all that God has said. The readers are sadly lacking in all that pertains to God's revelation.

The illustration of the use of milk (baby food) and solid food is found elsewhere (e.g., 1 Cor. 3:2, though with a different word for "food"). It is a graphic way of bringing out the difference between those who have made progress in the Christian faith and those whose growth has been stunted. The words "You need milk" more literally read "You have become having need of milk" (there is a similar construction in v. 11). Evidently the readers had first made progress but later had slipped back. Now, instead of being mature Christians, they have gone back to the stage where they depended on elementary nourishment, a sad state for those who should have been teachers.

With a negative and a positive the writer points to an important contrast. First the negative: the person who must be sustained by milk "is not acquainted with the teaching about righteousness" (v. 13). This may mean the teaching about the righteousness of God revealed in the gospel (Rom. 1:16–17), or it may mean teaching about the right conduct expected of believers. With a very different approach some hold that "righteousness" here is connected with the right way of speaking and see the expression simply as a way of carrying on the metaphor of infancy—the infant cannot understand even the right form of speech. This is not impossible, but it seems likely that we should take the words in the second sense.

The positive statement is that solid food is the food of mature people; this means Christians who have trained themselves "to distinguish good from evil" (v. 14). The readers were clearly being attracted by a form of conduct that was wrong for Christians. If they had made the progress in the faith that would have been expected, they would have been mature enough to have avoided that pitfall.

B. Exhortation to Progress (6:1–3)

Now comes a minor surprise. The writer has said that the readers have regressed to the infantile stage of wanting to be fed with milk. But he does not supply the beverage. He says, "Therefore let us leave the elementary teachings about Christ" (v. 1). "Therefore": precisely because they were in the position of infants.

His reasoning appears to be that these "elementary teachings" could find a place in the Jewish religion; to emphasize them at this stage might well have encouraged his readers to slip back quietly into Judaism. He refers, for example, to "the foundation of repentance" as a foundation that does not need to be laid again, and repentance was highly prized by the rabbis. He goes on to specify that repentance is "from acts that lead to death." With this we should take "faith in God," a faith that is constantly before us in this epistle. Elsewhere in the New Testament we commonly come across faith in Christ, but this writer mostly emphasizes faith in God. Actually there is not much difference, for if we really trust the Father we will certainly trust the Son and vice versa.

Next comes "instruction about baptisms" (v. 2). The plural makes it unlikely that Christian baptism is in mind and the word used is not the usual word for this baptism. Rather, it is used of various ceremonies of purification with water such as were common in the Jewish religion and in most other religions of the day (e.g., 9:10; Mark 7:4), and problems seem to have arisen quite early concerning such matters (John 3:25; Acts 19:1–5). Thus people needed instruction in the variety of "baptisms" they would meet from time to time. "The laying on of hands" was practiced in a variety of situations in antiquity. The Christians used it in more ways than one (Acts 6:6; 8:17–19; 9:17; 13:3; 1 Tim. 4:14; 2 Tim. 1:6), so that instruction in what it meant and in when and how it should be done was another early piece of teaching.

Both Jews and Christians firmly believed in "the resurrection of the dead, and eternal judgment." It is true that they understood these differently, but their common acceptance of these as realities set them apart from most people. It was clearly important that converts be given instruction in such matters. They would need to know why these two religions held such views and in what these views differed. They would need instruction in the fact that they were responsible men and women who one day would be raised from the dead and would have to give account of themselves to God. The writer rounds off this section of his argument with the declaration that they will go on to maturity "God permitting." He does not overlook the fact that God is in control.

C. No Second Beginning (6:4–8)

It is one of the basic things about the Christian way that we rarely stand still. We either progress in the faith or we slip back. The writer proceeds to make the point that people who turn away from the Christian faith cut themselves off from God's blessing. This passage is often taken to mean that a genuine Christian may slip back and thus commit a sin that cannot be forgiven. But we should be clear that this is not what the writer is saying: it is the impossibility of repentance of which he writes, not that of forgiveness. He speaks of people who have had enough experience of Christian things to know what the faith is all about. They have been "enlightened" (v. 4), a general term that certainly applies to Christians but also to some extent to all who have come in contact with Christianity. They have come to know something of the light that is Christ. So with "the heavenly gift"; it may mean the gift of saving faith, but the term is wide enough to cover any gift of God. To have "shared in the Holy Spirit" would be an appropriate way of referring to the experience of becoming a Christian, but the Spirit is at work far beyond the confines of the church in His works of "common grace." Indeed, "Every good and perfect gift is from above" (James 1:17), so that God is at work in many gifts given to people who are not Christians, as well as those who are. To have "tasted the goodness of the word of God and the powers of the coming age" (v. 5) means that the people in question knew enough about the Christian way to know that they ought to go on with it. Nothing in the passage says that genuine Christians may fall away and that if they do they may never come back. That would put this writer in contradiction with other New Testament writers who emphasize that people continue as Christians because of God's power and not because of their own efforts (e.g., John 6:39;

10:27–29). There is no real reason for holding that he is making such a contradiction.

The writer does not say that this falling away has happened, and some suggest that he is describing a hypothetical possibility by way of warning. But unless he is speaking of a real possibility his warning means nothing. It is much more likely that he has in mind a situation like that of Simon Magus in Acts 8. This man "believed and was baptized. And he followed Philip everywhere" (Acts 8:13). This is as definite as anything in Hebrews 6. But after all this it could be said of him, "your heart is not right before God . . . you are full of bitterness and captive to sin" (Acts 8:21–23). To know what the Christian experience is and to turn away from it is to repeat the mistake of Simon Magus. It is to take one's stand with those who put Jesus on the cross.

An illustration follows. Land that produces a crop "receives the blessing of God" (v. 7), but that which brings forth "thorns and thistles" is of no use and in the end will be the scene of burning (6:8). Land that produces no crops in the end can be nothing but the place of flames. And lives that do not respond to the love of God in Christ can end only in disaster.

D. Exhortation to Perseverance (6:9–12)

The warning has been blunt. The readers cannot miss the point that failure to go on with Jesus is serious and will result in irreparable loss. But that does not mean that the writer is unsure of his readers. On the contrary, he is "confident of better things . . . things that accompany salvation" (v. 9). It is important to make clear to them the issues that are involved. But it is also important to give them the encouragement they need, and the writer proceeds to do just that. He uses an affectionate form of address, "dear friends" (more literally, "beloved"), a form he uses only here in the epistle. He leaves them in no doubt as to his deep affection for them.

Verse 10 shows that his confidence rests in God, not in anything his readers can do. The NIV omits the word "For" at the beginning of this verse, but it is important. The writer is saying that the reason for his confidence in his friends is that "God is not unjust." God, being the kind of God He is, will never let His people down. The readers have produced "work" of some kind, and they have shown that they really love God by engaging in constant help of God's people. John points out that the person who shows no compassion on "his brother in need" does not really love God (1 John 3:17); anyone who "does not love his brother . . . cannot love God" (1 John 4:20). By this test the readers come out well. They have served others and they continue to serve them.

The writer desperately wants each and every one of his readers to persevere (v. 11). "We want" translates a very strong verb with a meaning like "to set one's heart upon." Notice the threefold evidence of his strong affection for them: "beloved" (v. 9), "we set our heart on" your perseverance, and "each of you." His reference to "this same diligence" implies that they had previously shown diligence; he simply wants to make sure that this continues to the end.

The end of the verse is not easy to translate; it has a meaning something like "to show the same diligence to the fullness of the hope until the end." The writer wants the readers' hope to be fully developed. Hope is an important quality in the New Testament and it is often linked with faith and love (e.g., 10:22–24; 1 Cor. 13:13). It is the blazing certainty of God's ultimate triumph; we can ill do without it. The readers had clearly manifested something of this hope and the writer has a strong desire to see its full development.

Hope is a spur to Christian activity. He wants them to have the fullness of hope so that they do not "become lazy" (v. 12). There is always a temptation to grow slack, and we have seen several indications in the letter so far that the readers had given cause for concern. Far from being lazy, the writer looks for his friends to imitate "those who through faith and patience inherit what has been promised." In other words, he points them to the examples of genuine believers who had preceded them. These believers had inherited the promises; the readers should imitate them. They are not simply to follow them, as those who come later in time. They are to do similar deeds, modeling themselves on these illustrious predecessors. The two qualities he singles out are faith and patience. Faith is basic to Christianity and receives emphasis throughout the New Testament, not least in this epistle (cf. chap. 11). But there are always difficulties in the path of the Christian and it is necessary to add the quality of steadfastness, which means not being deterred however great the difficulties. "Inherit" points to secure possession, and the reference to the promises shows that the final happy state is God's gift, not the result of human striving.

E. God's Promise Is Sure (6:13–20)

That it is God's gift gives it certainty, and the mention of the promises leads on to a consideration of the promise God made to Abraham. This patriarch is mentioned ten times in this epistle (the only New Testament writings with more references to him are John with eleven and Luke with fifteen); he will receive extended treatment when the author writes about faith (11:8–19). When God made a promise to Abraham He confirmed it with an oath, which itself shows that there would be quite a long time of waiting (had the carrying out of the promise been in the immediate future, there would have been no need of an oath). The point is that Abraham had a solemn promise from God, but nothing else. He had to wait in faith and for many years. In God's good time the promise was fulfilled, but until the fulfillment Abraham simply had to wait. The promise is given in general terms (v. 14, quoting Gen. 22:17; cf. Gen. 12:1–3) and simply assures the patriarch that he will have "many descendants." God says nothing about how or when. But Abraham waited patiently and in the end "received what was promised" (v. 15). Of course, he could not himself see the complete fulfillment of the promise. That required the appearance of the nation Israel. But he saw the beginnings and knew that God was doing what He had said He would do.

We should not underestimate the patience required of Abraham. The promise was made to him when he was seventy-five years old (Gen. 12:4), but he was a hundred when Isaac was born (Gen. 21:5), and Sarah was long past the age for normal childbearing. It needed patience and faith to believe through all these years. And it was another sixty years before Jacob and Esau were born (Gen. 25:26). But God had promised and what God promises He performs. So Abraham believed and lived to see the beginning of the fulfillment of the wonderful promise that had been made to him.

Now the author gives more attention to the oath. He has already said that God had no one greater by whom to swear so He swore by Himself (v. 13); he now points out that people generally swear oaths by someone greater than themselves (v. 16). The oath invokes punishment from the greater one if they do not carry out what they have vowed before him. This is the most solemn form of assertion we have and it has two results: it confirms what has been said (there is no going back on what has been solemnly sworn) and it ends all argument. In his reference to confirmation, the writer makes use of an expression found frequently in the papyri, which has something of the force of a legal guarantee. There is to be no doubt about the force of an oath.

This is why God swore an oath to Abraham. There was no necessity for an oath; God could have left it at a simple promise. The word translated "wanted" is related to "purpose" later in the verse (v. 17). The combination puts emphasis on the divine purpose, on the will of God at work. There is to be no doubt as to "the unchanging nature of his purpose." The word translated "confirmed" (found only here in the New Testament) has the force of a guarantee. The promise was enough, but it is guaranteed by the oath.

We should notice the further point that "the heirs of what was promised" can scarcely be Abraham or the other patriarchs. The promise in question could not be fulfilled in their days. The oath, of course, gave them certainty, but the fulfillment of the promise could be seen only in later times and this prepares us for the "we" of the next verse: the oath had reference to the days of the writer and his readers (and we may add, to ours).

The purpose of all this is to give encouragement to God's people. There are now "two unchangeable things in which it is impossible for God to lie"

(v. 18), the promise and the oath. The double assurance leaves no room for doubt. The divine purpose is plainly linked with the people of New Testament times, not just the ancients, for it is "we" who are to be "greatly encouraged." We "have fled," which points to the truth that Christians are people who have forsaken the illusory security of worldliness. They have run away from that security and have committed themselves to the God who has promised and sworn that He will give blessing.

They "take hold of the hope" that is offered to them and this hope is described as "an anchor for the soul" (v. 19). The anchor secures the ship; it prevents it from drifting where wind and tide might take it but where the captain does not wish to go. The metaphor of the anchor is often used in writings from antiquity, but it is used in the New Testament only in this passage. Hope gives firmness and security to Christians. It anchors us so that we do not drift here and there with the crosscurrents of this world. Almost inevitably translations refer to "the soul," and this is right, for hope does anchor the soul. But the word has a wider application, which is surely in mind here. The writer is not saying only that hope gives security to our "spiritual" lives; it gives security to all of life. In all that we do we are sustained by hope, that hope which is firmly grounded in the promise and the oath of God.

This is further brought out with the reference to hope entering "the inner sanctuary behind the curtain." In the tabernacle there was the small room behind the curtain called the "Most Holy Place," the place that people could not enter (except for the high priest on one day in the year), for it stood for the presence of God Himself. People could not enter, but hope can. It is a graphic way of saying that hope reaches out to the very presence of God. It reaches to the place "where Jesus, who went before us, has entered on our behalf" (v. 20). Our hope is based, not on anything of our own merit or devising, but on the sure promise and oath of God and on its fulfillment in the work that Christ has done for us. Later in the epistle the writer will bring out something of the significance of Jesus' going behind the curtain (e.g., 9:11–14). Here his point is simply that Jesus has gone into the presence of God on our behalf and that this gives us hope. There is another point. "Who went before us" is the translation of a noun with the meaning "forerunner," and "forerunner" implies later runners. There is no point in using the word if there is just the one runner. The word conveys the assurance that in due course we will be there, too. Jesus has entered on our behalf, and because He entered, one day we will enter as well.

Entrance into the Most Holy Place leads to the thought that Jesus "has become a high priest forever, in the order of Melchizedek." Our author has mentioned this in passing (5:6, 10). Now the time has come to bring out something of its significance. But that is another topic and another chapter.

For Further Study

1. Gather the passages that speak of the readers as not having progressed sufficiently in the Christian faith. What warning do these passages have for us today?

2. What passages can you find that speak of the security believers have? In the light of these, how are we to understand warnings against falling away?

3. What other passages can you find that link faith, hope, and love? How important are these three qualities for Christian living?

4. What does this passage teach us about hope?

5. What may we learn from this section of the epistle about the purposes of God?

Chapter 6

A Priest Like Melchizedek

(Hebrews 7:1–28)

Melchizedek is an enigmatic figure. He appears in the Old Testament in just one incident, namely when he met Abraham as the patriarch was coming back from a battle. We find that he was "priest of God Most High" as well as "king of Salem," that he brought out bread and wine, that he blessed Abraham, and that Abraham gave him a tenth of everything (Gen. 14:18–20). And that is all. He is also mentioned once in the Psalms (Ps. 110:4), but nowhere else in the Old Testament. He does not feature in Jewish literature, nor is he mentioned outside this epistle in the New Testament. Clearly most thinkers in antiquity found him a strange figure and they said nothing about him. But our author is able to show that a study of this somewhat obscure person tells us some important things about Christ and Christians.

A. The Greatness of Melchizedek (7:1–10)

The first point on which to be clear is that Melchizedek was no mean figure. He was both a king and a priest. This combination is found sometimes in antiquity, but it is not a feature of biblical life. "King of Salem" may mean "King of Jerusalem" (cf. Ps. 76:2), but if the author understood the term in this way we might have expected him to point out that Jesus died in that city. There is evidence that other places were also called by this name, and one of those may be meant. But our author is not specially interested in geography. It is the combination of royalty and priesthood that intrigues him and the meaning of the names. He speaks briefly of three things that happened: Melchizedek met Abraham as the patriarch returned from his victorious battle, he blessed him, and Abraham gave him a tenth of all the spoils. Then he goes right on to the meaning of the names.

The name Melchizedek, the writer says, means "king of righteousness." It could also be translated "My king is righteous," but the important thing is the connection with righteousness. "King of Salem" is then translated "king of peace." The Hebrew word *šālôm* means "peace," but peace in a full and rich sense. For the Hebrews, peace was not a negative term; it did not denote the absence of war, as with us, but the presence of positive blessing. It denoted wholeness, completeness, the well-rounded life that comes when we are right with God and God gives His rich blessing. The combination of righteousness and peace is found in a number of important passages (e.g., Ps. 85:10; Isa. 9:6–7; 32:17). It is important for the understanding of the Christian salvation (Rom. 5:1), which may be why the author brings it out.

The terms "without father" and "without mother" (v. 3) were used in a variety of ways in the Greek of that time. Homeless children were described in this way, as were the illegitimate or those whose birth was into some far-from-aristocratic family. But no such usage helps us with the present passage. Some draw attention to the use of these terms to describe certain deities who were thought to have had only one parent. They go on from there to suggest that the writer thinks of Melchizedek as an angel or the like. But more probably we are presented with an example of exegesis not uncommon among the Jews, in which the silences of Scripture are considered inspired and significant. This approach seems strange to us, but people in antiquity used it. For example, Philo uses the exact term found here, "without mother," of Sarah. He speaks of her as "the virtue-loving mind" (he was an incurable allegorist), and says that she was "declared . . . to be without a mother," because her mother is not mentioned in Genesis 20:12. She was not born "of perceptible matter, always forming and dissolving . . . but from the Cause and Father of all" (*On Drunkenness*, 59–61).

Not only is Melchizedek without father or mother, but he is "without genealogy, without beginning of days or end of life." For a priest to be without genealogy was most extraordinary, as we see clearly from an incident at the end of the Exile, when certain people who claimed to be priests were excluded from priestly functions because their genealogy was not attested (Neh. 7:64). To be without a genealogy was to be excluded from the priesthood. But Melchizedek is a most unusual person: of him no father is recorded, no mother, no ancestors (or for that matter descendants), no beginning or end to his life.

The point of all this is that he is "made like unto the Son of God" (KJV). We should not make the mistake of thinking that Melchizedek is the standard and that Jesus was made like him. It is the other way around. It is the priesthood of Christ that is the standard. The silences of Scripture help us see some important things about Christ's priesthood. What is simply the absence of record in the case of Melchizedek points us to what is literal fact in the case of Christ. A study of Melchizedek helps us to see something of what is meant by the eternal priesthood Christ exercises.

The writer continues his treatment of Melchizedek to bring out the superiority of Christ's priesthood to any other, specifically to that of Aaron. Melchizedek is shown by the Law to be superior to Aaron, so that a priest like Melchizedek is superior to any Aaronic priest. Again, Abraham gave Melchizedek a tenth of the spoils of war (v. 4). It was a Jewish practice that Israelites paid their tithes to Levi's descendants, but Levi, our author reasons, was in a sense included in Abraham ("Levi was still in the body of his ancestor," v. 10) when Abraham paid his tenth. Thus the Aaronic priesthood symbolically recognized the superiority of Melchizedek. With this is intertwined an argument from the fact that Melchizedek blessed Abraham, and there is no doubt but that "the lesser person is blessed by the greater" (v. 7). In Israel it was mortal men who collected tithes, but in Melchizedek's case it was done by "him who is declared to be living" (v. 8). The whole incident leaves no doubt, our author reasons, but that Melchizedek was far superior to any other priest, and specifically to those who descended from Aaron (and who were so greatly revered by the Jews).

B. The Royal Priesthood of Melchizedek and of Christ (7:11–14)

It is basic for our author that the priesthood that the Jews valued so highly and the Law that they revered so devoutly could not do what they thought. This priesthood and this Law were powerless to deal with people's real needs. The writer denies that they can bring about "perfection," the quality of making sinners acceptable to God (v. 11). Notice that he links the Law and the priesthood. We should not think of these as two unrelated parts of Israelite life. They were closely connected. The priesthood was laid down in the Law and the Law could not be fully carried out without the priesthood. The priesthood was regulated in the Law and could not be exercised, at least not in the way God intended, apart from the Law. The writer has already argued that the superiority of Melchizedek's priesthood is shown in the Law, for it is in the Law and in the Law alone that we read of the incident with Abraham. Now he goes on to argue that the passage in Psalm 110 is important. It cannot be urged that Aaron came later than Melchizedek and thus was intended by God to supersede the earlier priest. For Psalm 110 is later than the Law; indeed, it was composed after the Aaronic priesthood had been functioning for hundreds of years. And this psalm clearly speaks of the validity of the priesthood like that of Melchizedek. So at this point the writer refers to the "need for another priest to come," and a little later he will quote the psalm again and speak of the setting aside of the regulation that made Aaron and his line priests (vv. 17–18). Out of the Scriptures in which the Jews put so much trust it can be demonstrated that the Aaronic priesthood is not God's final word.

The argument of verse 11 then is that the very existence of the reference in the Psalms to a priest like Melchizedek shows that the Levitical priesthood could not effect the "perfection" at which it aimed. That means that there must be a change of priesthood and, because priesthood and the Law went together, a change in the Law as well (v. 12). The whole system into which the readers were tempted to slip back was shown by its own Scriptures to be inadequate.

Now Jesus belonged to the tribe of Judah, the royal tribe of David and the kings, not the tribe of priests (vv. 13–14). No one from Judah was ever a priest. Moses said nothing about priests when he was talking about that tribe. To speak of Jesus as a priest, then, was to speak of something completely new. His priesthood was certainly envisaged in the ancient Scripture, as the references to Melchizedek plainly show. But Jesus is not to be fitted comfortably into the Jewish system. For the Jews the one priesthood was that in the line of Aaron. For the Christians the one priesthood is that of Christ; the Aaronic priesthood must be rejected because it could not bring about the "perfection" at which it aimed. Thus there must be a completely new start, and a priesthood from a totally different source shows that the new start has been made.

C. Christ's Priesthood Is Superior (7:15–28)

The writer develops the thought that the priesthood of Christ is superior to any other priesthood. Melchizedek helps us see some of the essential things about the final priesthood, and bit by bit the writer builds up his case that Christ is inherently superior to any other priest. He has accomplished a work of salvation that completely meets the needs of sinners, whereas the Aaronic priesthood cannot do that.

1. *Superior because of His life* (7:15–19)

There is nothing in the Greek to correspond to the NIV's "what we have said"; it reads simply, "And it is even more clear." The NIV may be correct, but some see the "even more clear" thing as the doing away of the priesthood, others as the demolishing of the place of the Law. In the end we must remain uncertain, but the main point is clear—the coming of a priest like Melchizedek has changed everything.

This priest was made a priest "not on the basis of a regulation as to his ancestry but on the basis of the power of an indestructible life" (v. 16). Here the translators of the NIV have decided that the "law of a fleshly commandment" (which is what the Greek means) is to be understood with reference to ancestry. The NEB has "a system of earth-bound rules," which is wider but still does not take into account the reference to "fleshly." The writer is including all that refers to this life in the flesh, all that the commandments in the old Law could embrace; the expression is broad enough to cover all the situations of this life. But Jesus is not bound by the situations of this life. His life is of a different order. It is "indestructible."

This does not mean only that His life *does* not end—it means that it *cannot* end. It is of a different quality. Jesus does not stand in the same relation to life as we do. We do not live by virtue of any inherent necessity, but He is "the Prince of life" (Acts 3:15, KJV)—He lives and must live.

The writer quotes Psalm 110:4 again to emphasize this point. The priesthood of Christ, like that of Melchizedek, is "forever." It does not depend on any commandment that has to do with the affairs of the here and now. His life is "indestructible." Thus there is no end and there can be no end to His priesthood.

The earlier regulation "is set aside," where we have a legal term with the meaning "annulment." The regulation has been called "fleshly" (v. 16) and to that is now added "it was weak and useless" (v. 18). The old system with its priests and its sacrifices could point people to the right way but it could never meet the deep needs of their souls. This does not mean that in Old Testament times people did not find peace with God. They certainly did, as is attested again and again. To take but one example, the Twenty-third Psalm is a wonderful expression of trust and peace and to this day the people of God use it with gratitude and devotion. But the writer's point is that this kind of peace with God was not the result of the Levitical priesthood. That priesthood had its place in God's scheme of things and the author recognizes this from time to time (e.g., 9:13; 10:3). But it did not meet people's deepest needs and for that reason it had to be temporary. In the end there had to be the "annulment" of which he speaks here.

He explains further that "the law made nothing perfect" (v. 19). Neither here nor anywhere else does he explain what he means by "make perfect," but it is quite plain that he is referring to the Law's inability to make people fit to stand in God's presence. Sin stains us and separates us from God. The Levitical priesthood could provide sacrifices that reminded worshipers of the seriousness of sin and provided ceremonial cleansing, but it could not take those sins away and make the worshipers fit for the presence of God. It could not provide that which the worshipers needed above all.

But now "a better hope is introduced." We have already seen that hope is an important concept for our author, and for that matter for Christians in all ages. It ranks with faith and love as one of the three things that last forever (1 Cor. 13:13). So to people whom the Law had left without hope, hope is given, a hope that is better than the annulled regulation. The writer is fond of the idea that in the new system there are "better" things (see the list in the comments on 1:4).

Here he speaks of the better hope as that "by which we draw near to God." It was this that made the new system so wonderful and justified the use of the adjective "better." The old way had its merits but it could not bring people to God; the new way in Christ does. Christ is accordingly inherently and infinitely superior to all the Levitical priests.

2. *Superior because of the divine oath* (7:20–22)

We have been reminded of the divine oath that certain sinners would not enter God's rest (3:11, 18; 4:3) and of God's oath to Abraham (6:13–17). Now we have the thought that it is an oath that guarantees the permanency of Christ's priesthood. Once again the writer quotes Psalm 110:4, but this time he starts his quotation a little earlier to include the words, "The Lord has sworn and will not change his mind." The priesthood like that of Melchizedek is one established by a divine oath. There could be no firmer guarantee that it will never be changed.

There could be the thought in the mind of some readers that if the priesthood of Christ superseded that of Aaron, then it was reasonable to expect that one day the priesthood of Christ might be superseded by some other priesthood. Not so, reasons our author. The priesthood of Christ was established on the basis of a divine oath. God does not change His mind, and since He has so emphatically set up this new priesthood, we may rely on the fact that it will never be superseded. Christ is God's final word to mankind.

The fact of the oath leads on to another thought. Because of the oath, Jesus has become "the guarantee," an unusual thought, expressed with an unusual word (found only here in the New Testament). There is a twofold application. Obviously and in the first place, the oath makes Jesus God's guarantee to us. God has sworn that Jesus will be a priest forever. Those who come to God through Him and through what He has done are therefore guaranteed their place. The human name Jesus points us to the work our Savior did during His time on earth. It was on the cross that He consummated His priestly work and brought about the salvation that comes to us with the divine guarantee.

There is probably also the thought that He guarantees us to God. Clothed in the righteousness He provides, we are, as the hymn writer puts it, "Faultless to stand before the throne." He guarantees it.

This is the first time the writer uses the word "covenant," a word he will use seventeen times in all (out of the thirty-three times it is used in the New Testament). It is thus one of his major concepts and one that is much more prominent in this epistle than in any other New Testament writing. There is a problem as to its meaning. It is the usual word in secular Greek for "will" or "testament," the document in which a person makes the arrangements he desires for the disposal of his goods after his death. But this same word is used in the Septuagint to translate the Hebrew word for "covenant." In earlier days, the meaning "testament" was accepted, and this appears on the title pages of our Bibles as we refer to "the Old Testament" and "the New Testament." There can be no doubt that sometimes the word has this meaning in the New Testament (e.g., 9:16). Most, however, agree that usually the meaning is "covenant," for we must hold that in this matter the way the word is used in the Septuagint is decisive. Where God is making a covenant, the usual Greek word for "covenant" would not be appropriate (and is never used in the New Testament), because it lends itself to a situation in which the two parties dicker with each other so that each may get the best terms possible. But when God makes a covenant He lays down the terms. We cannot "trade" with God to get a better deal. We take it or leave it, just as is the case when a testator makes a bequest on certain conditions. The word that meant a final and authoritative laying down of the terms was much more suitable for a covenant into which God entered. So, though the word is not the usual one in Greek for "covenant," we can safely accept this as the meaning, with the reservation that there will be occasions when "testament" is a better rendering.

"Covenant" here then stands for the whole way of approach to God revealed in the Old Testament (the writings of the Old Covenant). This is replaced by the new way, a better covenant. And Jesus is the Guarantor of this new covenant. From yet another angle the superiority of His priesthood is brought out.

3. *Superior because of its permanence* (7:23–25)

The oath has shown that the priesthood of Christ is permanent. There will be no change, ever. But the writer brings out the same point in another way, by showing that the multiplicity of priests in the Levitical system is significant. There had to be many Levitical priests "since death prevented them from continuing in office" (v. 23). A dead priest may inspire by reason of a recollection of the excellence of his life, but he can no longer do anything to effect the removal of sin. His usefulness is over. The fact of death means a limitation on the work of such priests.

But Jesus "lives forever" (v. 24). His priesthood is not limited like that of the descendants of Aaron. He is always there; His priesthood is everlastingly effective. The word translated "permanent" (found only here in the New Testament) means "that cannot be transgressed," "inviolable," and so "unchangeable." The continuing life of Jesus gives a continuing validity to His priesthood.

And that has its consequences for the salvation He brings (v. 25). He "is able," which points to His unlimited power. "To save" is used absolutely; there is no qualification such as "save from sin" or "save into glory." It embraces all that salvation can include. "Completely" translates another unusual expression, found elsewhere in the New Testament only of the woman who was bent over and could not straighten herself "at all" (Luke 13:11); it means "totally," "completely." Jesus brings a salvation that lacks nothing. It is complete. He saves totally. He saves "those who come to God through him" (which excludes universalism).

At the end of the verse is a statement of Christ's perpetual intercession. Christians have always found it a precious thought that there is no end to and no cessation of the intercession that is made on their behalf. In our sinful state we cannot but feel that we need such intercession. At the same time, the intercession must be understood carefully and taken with other passages, such as those that speak of Christ as seated at God's right hand. We have already noticed that this points to the thought of a finished work, a work completed when Christ died for sinners on Calvary (cf. comments on 1:3). Now He is in the highest place in heaven in glory. He is not to be thought of as perpetually on His knees or standing with hands outstretched to God. He is on the throne and His presence is itself an intercession. To put it anthropomorphically, every time the Father looks at His Son He can say, "This is my beloved Son who died for sinners." His presence, in His capacity as the crucified and risen and ascended One, is itself a perpetual intercession.

4. *Superior because of His better sacrifice* (7:26–28)

The NIV omits the word "For," which should begin verse 26. It is an important connective: the writer introduces the reason for the effectiveness of Christ's intercession. That intercession prevails *because* Christ is the wonderful High Priest He is. With a lesser person it would be impossible. But He "meets our need" (i.e., He is eminently suited to provide salvation for all who come to God through Him). Now comes a list of qualities that mark Him out. First, He is "holy," God's "Holy One" (cf. Acts 2:27; 13:35), righteous in all His ways. With that goes "blameless" (no accusation could be fairly leveled at Him) and "pure." This last word signifies "undefiled" and may point us to the assiduous pursuit of ritual cleanliness that was the constant preoccupation of the Levitical high priest, who always had to be on his guard to make sure that nothing defiled him and thus prevented him from carrying out his important duties. But Jesus went through this earthly life, living in the same circumstances as all men must, constantly assailed by temptation (4:15), but remaining "undefiled." His purity was a moral purity quite unstained throughout His earthly life, and this stands in marked contrast to the merely ritual purity by which the descendants of Aaron set such store.

He is "set apart from sinners," which must be understood carefully. He is not withdrawn from them as one who says, "I am holier than thou." Nor is He separate in the sense of living a life without contact with sinners and with temptation. The Gospels show us the falsity of any such idea. He is separate in the sense that He did not sin as they did. He is separate also in the sense that His earthly pilgrimage has ended and that He is now "exalted above the heavens." This way of speaking puts emphasis on the truth that He is in the highest place of all.

The Levitical high priests were under the necessity of making constant offerings for themselves before they could offer for others (v. 27). They were sinners and had to be cleansed from their sins before they could be deemed worthy to offer sacrifices for other people. There is a minor problem in that in the temple organization as we know it the high priest did not offer the daily sacrifices; this was normally done by the ordinary priests. But this verse speaks of need, and it may be that the Levitical high priest, being a sinner like everyone else, had a daily need to offer sacrifice if he was to be fit to minister in the holy things that belonged to his office. We should remember also that the high priest was to offer the cereal offering every day (Lev. 6:19–23). What is emphasized is that the earthly high priest was a sinful man: he needed daily cleansing and there was a continual round of sacrifices to bring this about.

But Christ, by contrast, does not need a sacrifice for Himself, and furthermore, He offered His sacrifice of Himself "once for all." The thought that the sacrifice Christ offered was "once for all" is an important one and the writer brings it out repeatedly (9:12, 26, 28; 10:10). It stands in marked contrast to the daily Levitical sacrifices and even the yearly Day of Atonement offerings. The one sacrifice of Christ effectively took away sin. When that was done there was no need or place for any further sacrifice. That He offered a sacrifice so much better than any Levitical sacrifice is a further indication of the superiority of Christ's priesthood to any other.

This section of the argument is rounded off with a number of points that further emphasizes the superiority of Christ. First, the priests appointed under the Law are "men who are weak" (v. 28). The term has reference to physical weakness, but also to moral frailty. The descendants of Aaron were not a group of superlative saints; they were weak and imperfect sinners. The Son, by contrast, "has been made perfect forever." He has come right where sinners are, has kept Himself free from sin, has offered the perfect sacrifice, has been made perfect through suffering (2:10), and remains in that state of perfection.

There is also a contrast between the Law and the oath. Christ's priesthood, being like that of Melchizedek, already has a place in the Law. But it is also confirmed by the oath, centuries after the Law. The Law cannot be said to supersede the oath; rather, it is the other way around. More than once our author appeals to the Psalms to indicate that God's word is subsequent to the Law. So is it here: the Son is appointed by the divine oath well after the Law had been given and put into operation. This gives an air of finality to His priesthood. Once we have considered the implications of the priesthood like that of Melchizedek, it is impossible to be impressed by the Aaronic priesthood. It has been comprehensively replaced.

For Further Study

1. Read the story of Melchizedek in Genesis 14:18–20 and the reference to him in Psalm 110. List all that the Old Testament tells us about him.

2. In what ways does our author show the greatness of Melchizedek?
3. In what respects is the priesthood of Jesus like that of Melchizedek?
4. In what ways does a consideration of Melchizedek show the superiority of Jesus' priesthood to that of the Aaronic priests?
5. What do we learn from this chapter about the character of Jesus?

Chapter 7

A New and Better Covenant (I)

(Hebrews 8:1–9:28)

We have seen that the concept of covenant was a very significant one for the Jews. It dominated their thinking. The most important thing in all of life for them was that God stood in a special relationship to this one nation. He was their God; they were His people. This put them in a very special place, since there is no other god. Their whole way of life was organized around this central theme. Their Scriptures were given them by their covenant God and contained His will for them. They regulated their lives by what they found there and their whole way of worship and of living sprang from the deep conviction of their special place in God's plan. The covenant made them what they were.

Thus when the writer of this epistle speaks of the covenant as "obsolete" (8:13), he is not making an observation of minor importance; he is striking at the heart of the Jewish understanding of God's ways with men. To him it was of critical importance that the covenant on which the Jews relied so wholeheartedly was ineffective. In the section of the epistle we have just studied he insists that the Aaronic priesthood is "weak and useless" (7:18); it must be replaced by the priesthood of Christ, a priesthood like that of Melchizedek. He will go on to argue that the sacrifices of the old covenant cannot take away sin and that sin can be removed only by the sacrifice that Christ offered, the sacrifice of Himself.

A. Christ's "More Excellent" Ministry (8:1–7)

He begins this section of his argument by drawing attention to the chief point in what has gone before—the fact and the nature of Christ's priesthood. He has just spoken of the Son as the perfect High Priest, a High Priest appointed by a divine oath so that His priesthood is forever. Now he goes on to say, "We do have such a high priest" (v. 1), and adds a point he has made previously: He "sat down at the right hand of the throne of the Majesty in heaven" (cf. 1:3). He thus introduces his "new covenant" theme by reminding his readers of Christ's finished work ("sat down"), and of His being in the place of highest honor in heaven. As in 1:3, God is referred to as "the Majesty" and His royal state is emphasized with the reference to "the throne" (which is not mentioned in 1:3, but is found again in 12:2).

The mention of heaven leads on to the thought that Christ's service is more than merely earthly, as the service of the Aaronic priests was (v. 2). Christ is called "a servant" (NIV, "who serves"); the word is one that is always used in the Bible of the service of God, though in nonbiblical writings it sometimes refers to the service of men. It may be used of pagans (e.g., Rom. 13:6), but it is always service of God that is in mind. In this way it is used of angels (1:7) as well as of men (Rom. 15:16). Christ serves in "the sanctuary," which is defined as "the true tabernacle" and further explained as "set up by the Lord, not by man." Up to this point we have had some references to the Israelites in the wilderness, but this is the first specific reference to the tabernacle, the tent that was the center of Israel's worship. But our author is clear that "the true" tabernacle is not that tent; it is one set up by God. The thought is not developed at this point, but the writer will come back to it later (9:23–24). Here he does no more than note the location as a way of rounding off his point that Christians have a high priest whose work is effective where it counts.

It is of the essence of priesthood and, of course, of high priesthood, "to offer both gifts and sacrifices" (v. 3). It is this that differentiates the priest from the lay person. It is the heart of the priestly ministry. There are other things a priest does, many of which lay people do as well. But the offering of sacrifice is the central thing. Without that a man is not a priest. Thus our author can argue that it was "necessary" that Christ have something to offer. If we are to see Him as a priest, then it is essential that we see Him as offering a sacrifice. Without that He is no priest. What the offering is the writer does not say at this stage. It is characteristic of him simply to mention it and to come back to it later (cf. chap. 10). The way he expresses himself here points to a single offering and not the daily offerings of the Levitical priests, but we cannot say more.

He has said that Christ's priesthood is in heaven, and he now goes on to point out that it *has* to be. On earth He would not be a priest, for there are priests here who make the earthly offerings (v. 4). Notice that it is His priesthood, not His offering, that is in heaven, for His offering took place on Calvary. Jesus came from the tribe of Judah, not that of Levi (cf. 7:13–14), so He did not offer the sacrifice laid down by the Law. But these earthly priests do not minister where the action really is. They serve "at a sanctuary that is a copy and shadow of what is in heaven" (v. 5).

There has been much dispute as to the extent to which our author has been influenced by Greek philosophy at this point. Plato taught that the perfect "idea" or "form" of everything is in heaven and that all we ever see on earth are imperfect copies or shadows of the heavenly realities, which is much like the distinction the writer is making here. But others point out that there is a strand of Jewish thinking that insists that there are things on earth that are the copies of things in heaven. For example, there is a prayer that says, "Thou hast given command to build a temple on thy holy mountain, and an altar in the city of thy habitation, a copy of the holy tent which thou didst prepare from the beginning" (Wisdom of Solomon 9:8). The author of Hebrews gives no indication that he is a learned philosopher, but on the other hand, he does not say, as Jewish writers did, that the earthly sanctuary was a copy of the heavenly. Perhaps he is indebted to both strands to express a thought that is his own.

His point is that the ministry of the Aaronic priests is defective because their ministry cannot operate in what he has called "the true tabernacle" (v. 2). It is, and can be, only in the "copy and shadow" of the heavenly reality. He goes on to quote Exodus 25:40, where Moses was instructed to make the tabernacle "according to the pattern" he had been shown on the mountain. This implies that the earthly tabernacle is somewhat like the heavenly, but also that it is not in fact the heavenly one. We can learn some important truths from the earthly tabernacle (as we do, for example, in 9:6–9). But the effective ministry that really puts away sin cannot take place there. That must be done in "the true tabernacle."

This leads inevitably to the thought that Jesus' ministry is superior to that of the Aaronic priests (v. 6). We might perhaps have expected that he would develop this thought with respect to the sanctuaries in which they ministered. But the sanctuaries are no more than an introduction to the topic the writer is about to develop—the superiority of the new covenant to the old. The true tabernacle and its copy form a useful introduction to a demonstration that the new covenant far outclasses the old. The ministry and the covenant go together; in the case of both, what Jesus has done is effective, whereas what the Aaronic priests have done, and continue to do, is not.

The writer goes on to say that the new covenant "is founded on better promises." As the subsequent discussion will show, he is primarily concerned with the promises of forgiveness of sins, the forgiveness that is central in the Christian gospel. Such promises are found in the passage in Jeremiah that looks forward to the making of the new covenant. The defectiveness of the first covenant is seen in the very existence of the prophecy of the new covenant. Quite reasonably the writer points out that had there been "nothing wrong" with that older covenant there would have been no need to think of another (v. 7). But there is no getting around the fact that in the Scriptures to which the Jews appealed there is the prophecy that one day God will make a new covenant. Why? Because the old covenant was not working.

B. The Old Covenant Superseded (8:8–13)

The writer uses quite a long quotation from Jeremiah 31 to make his point that God has promised a new covenant, one that would bring significant changes. He introduces the quotation with the words, "But God found fault with the people" (v. 8). That was the trouble with the old covenant. The people had spontaneously agreed to obey all that the Lord commanded (Exod. 24:3, 7). But it is easier to say than to do, and Israel fell down on the job. Because of this failure a new arrangement became necessary, and the Lord says that He "will make a new covenant." The word for "make" is not the usual word for "making" a covenant; it stresses completion, as though to say, "I will bring a new covenant to fulfillment." The new arrangement will be brought about wholly by God Himself. Notice the reference to both "the house of Israel" and that "of Judah," which brings out the inclusiveness of the new covenant. It has, in fact, embraced more people by far than the old one did.

God's compassion in the making of the first covenant comes before us in the picture of His taking the people "by the hand to lead them out of Egypt" (v. 9). It is the imagery of a father leading his small child (cf. Hos. 11:1–4). God had tenderly delivered His people from their condition of slavery in Egypt and had brought them into their own land. But, though the people had had such clear evidence of God's love for them, "they did not remain faithful to my covenant," more literally, they did not remain "in" my covenant, which left it an empty shell. Perhaps this is why God speaks of a "new" covenant and not of restoring the covenant. What is envisaged is not an arrangement very much like the old one, but something completely new. Their failure to remain in the old covenant meant that "I turned away from them"—the inevitable response. There was no way forward via the old covenant.

From the old and its failure we turn to the new and its very different characteristics. The repeated "declares the Lord" (v. 10; cf. v. 8) emphasizes that the new covenant makes its appearance as the result of a divine initiative. It is what God has planned, not what man devises. The first point to be stressed is its inwardness. There had been tablets of stone associated with the old covenant and God's commandments were written on them (Exod. 32:15–16). These formed an impressive record of what God wanted the people to do, but the commandments were outside the people; they did not form part of them. In the new covenant God says, "I will put my laws in their minds and write them on their hearts." In this context "minds" and "hearts" do not differ markedly: they are both ways of saying that the new covenant is inward. It is not a matter of obeying an external code. It is a matter of making God's commands part of us. This means accepting them so that they shape our thinking and we want to live in accordance with them. Those who have God's laws in their hearts are different people from those who see those laws simply as a series of commandments that are to be obeyed in an external fashion.

The result of this change is that God and God's people are bound together in an intimate relationship. In a sense there is nothing new about this, for from of old, Israel had been the people of God and God had been their God (Exod. 6:7). But the prophets looked forward to something new (cf. Ezek. 11:20), and it is the coming of Jesus that makes all things new. His incarnation, His death and resurrection and ascension give a new meaning to being the people of God. We are now people who have been loved with the love we see on Calvary. We are people who have been died for. God is our God in the sense that we know that He is love (1 John 4:8, 16). There is a deeper meaning in being the people of God.

One result of this new relationship is a more intimate knowledge of God (v. 11). If God's laws are written within people, then those people have a knowledge of the God who wrote them: they have been taught by God (John 6:45; 1 Thess. 4:9) and they do not need others to teach them (1 John 2:20, 27). While it is always true that there are some who make better use of God's good gifts than others and who know more of God than others and can thus teach others about God, it is also true that in the new covenant there is no elite class of mediators who must be approached if ordinary people are to know about God and draw near to Him. The way into the Most Holy Place is wide open (10:19–20). In principle there is nothing to hinder the humblest of God's people from a most intimate knowledge of God. Indeed, through the centuries it has often been uneducated and insignificant people who have had the deepest faith and the closest walk with God. God looks for a time when all His people will know Him "from the least of them to the greatest."

And this will be possible because sin will no longer be a barrier. "I will forgive their wickedness and will remember their sins no more" (v. 12). The new covenant is not based on some commitment on the part of the people to be perfect in their obedience to all the commands of God. It is based on forgiveness. The cross is at the heart of the Christian way and the cross speaks of the love that brought forgiveness. When Christians sin there is no need for a fresh sacrifice. The one sacrifice once offered keeps the new covenant in force. It puts the sin away. God remembers sin no more.

The word "new" is important (v. 13). For our writer, every word of God is important and effectual. When God speaks of a new covenant it means that He has made the old covenant "obsolete." It is not possible to have a new covenant and an old one operating side by side. "Obsolete" means more than old; it means "worn out," "having lost its force." It means "aging" and therefore on its way out. It "will soon disappear." It is thus clear that the writer does not envisage the Jewish system as continuing as a viable option alongside the Christian way. It is his conviction that God has done a new thing in Christ. He has replaced the old way with a new way based on forgiveness and inwardness. There is no longer a reason for holding to the old way. It is obsolete, it is aging, it will soon disappear.

C. The Old Sanctuary and Its Ritual (9:1–10)

Throughout this section we must bear in mind the writer's deep conviction that the Jewish way, into which his readers were tempted to slip back, has been superseded. He does not see it as an acceptable alternative to Christianity. Anyone who would obey God must go forward with Christ, not backward to Moses. So he builds up his argument that from a variety of standpoints it is possible to see the inferiority of the old way.

He begins with a consideration of the way the tabernacle was set up. He does not refer to the temple (which was in Jerusalem and accessible only to those in the vicinity), nor to the synagogue (which is not found in the Old Testament). But all those who read the ancient Scripture would know of the tabernacle, and he can thus refer to it with confidence. He begins by pointing to the undoubted fact that in the first covenant there were "regulations for worship and also an earthly sanctuary" (v. 1). In these regulations and in the instructions for the setting up of the sanctuary God had told the Israelites what to do. It is thus important to take notice of what He has done. That the sanctuary is "earthly" is probably meant in contrast to the heavenly sanctuary in which Christ ministers (v. 11).

There is nothing in the Greek to correspond to the NIV's "its" and "room" (v. 2). The writer says, "A tabernacle (or, tent) was set up, the first in which were. . . ." He uses the same word for "tent" in verse 3, where the NIV again has "room." But the word does not mean "room"; he is speaking of two tents and says that in the first tent there were certain articles of furniture. The "lampstand" is the seven-branched lampstand of which we read so often (e.g., Exod. 25:31–40; 37:17–24). There were ten lampstands in Solomon's temple (1 Kings 7:49), but, of course, the writer is describing the tabermacle, not the temple. For "the table and the consecrated bread" see Leviticus 24:5–9; Numbers 4:7–8, etc. The writer does not describe the place or its furnishings in any greater detail, but contents himself with telling us that it was called "the Holy Place."

Then he turns to "the Most Holy Place" (which we more usually call "the Holy of Holies"), which he speaks of as a tent "behind the second curtain" (v. 3). It was the second curtain because there was a first curtain that separated the Holy Place from the outer court (Exod. 26:36–37). The Most Holy Place was to be entered only by the high priest and then only once a year, as the writer will emphasize in due course. For the present he is content to give its name and then to proceed to some of its furnishings. He speaks first of "the golden altar of incense" or, as the KJV has it, "the golden censer" (v. 4). The Greek clearly refers to something connected with incense, but without saying exactly what ("the incense thing"). In its infrequent occurrences in the Septuagint the word always means a censer, but there seems no reason for referring to a censer here, nor has a censer any special connection with the Most Holy Place. Most therefore accept "altar of incense." This altar stood outside the curtain (Exod. 30:6), not in the Most Holy Place. But then our author does not say that it was inside. He says that the Most Holy Place "had" it. It stood just outside the Most Holy Place and its use was bound up with what that place signified; it "belonged to the inner sanctuary" (1 Kings 6:22).

The "gold-covered ark of the covenant" was in the Most Holy Place in the tabernacle (Exod. 26:33; its construction is described in Exod. 25:10–22). It was also there in the temple at first (1 Kings 8:6), but at some unmentioned time and for some unexplained reason it was taken out. In the last reference we have to the ark, Josiah told the Levites to put it in the temple, adding, "It is not to be carried about on your shoulders" (2 Chron. 35:3). Nobody knows what happened to it after that, but somewhere in history it disappeared. There is a story that Jeremiah hid it (2 Maccabees 2:4–8), which seems very improbable. But for our author the present whereabouts of the ark do not matter. He is concerned with the way the tabernacle had been set up and with what we can learn from that.

From the ark the writer turns to its contents. He speaks first of "the gold jar of manna." Our Hebrew text does not say what the jar was made of (see Exod. 16:33–34), but the Septuagint says it was made of gold. The writer mentions also Aaron's rod that budded (Num. 17:1–11). These were closely associated with the ark, but in the Old Testament neither is said to have been in it: they were in front of it (Exod. 16:34; Num. 17:10). In the temple there was nothing in the ark but the stone tablets (1 Kings 8:9), but it may have been somewhat different in the tabernacle. Delitzsch argues that the terms of the statement in 1 Kings 8:9 may imply that other things had been in the ark earlier and he goes on to cite Jewish authorities who held that the jar of manna and the rod that budded were in the ark. In any case, nothing in the argument depends on the precise location of these objects and the writer expressly says that he is not going into detail (v. 5). He further mentions "the stone tablets of the covenant" (Deut. 9:9–11; 10:3–5). These contained the most sacred of the sacred writings and naturally were kept in the most sacred place.

The cover of the ark was of pure gold (Exod. 25:17) and at each end was a golden cherub. The precise form of a cherub is not known, but clearly wings were involved, for these overshadowed the cover as the cherubim faced each other. This feature of the tabernacle was very important, for God says, "There, above the cover between the two cherubim that are over the ark of the Testimony, I will meet with you" (Exod. 25:22; see also Pss. 80:1; 99:1; for the construction of the cover and the cherubim, see Exod. 25:17–22). The cover is here called "the place of atonement," which points to the fact that each year on the great Day of Atonement the high point of the day's observance was the sprinkling of the blood in front of and on this cover (Lev. 16:14, 15). The writer simply lists these articles and concludes by saying that he cannot go into detail. He has said enough to indicate the importance of the tabernacle furnishings, which is all that he needs.

He goes on to point out the significance of the arrangement as the priests went about their ministry (v. 6). They worked only in "the first tent" (the NIV has "outer room"; cf. vv. 2, 3). There they did things like trimming the lamps (Exod. 27:20–21), burning incense (Exod. 30:7–8), and setting out the holy loaves (Lev. 24:5–9). They moved quite freely in this area. This was a high privilege and even the Levites were on a lower plane (Num. 18:1–7).

But the important part of the argument concerns the high priest. Clearly the writer is here speaking about what happened on the Day of Atonement, for it was on that day and on that day alone in all the year that the high priest entered the Most Holy Place (v. 7); moreover, "only the high priest" entered that little room. It symbolized the very presence of God. People must keep their distance. Even priests could not enter it. The high priest himself was not allowed to enter it except for this one day in the year, and on that one day in the year even he could not enter "without blood." The writer sees it as important that the holiness of God be respected. Sinful people had to recognize that their sins had separated them from God and that they had no rights of access into His presence. But God is gracious and He provided the means whereby the representative of the people might take due precautions and then enter His presence for the purpose of making atonement for the sins of the people. Symbolically, the whole observance showed that God willed to have sin dealt with and to have His people come near to Him. But the whole rite was symbolic. Animals could not really put away sin and the people's access to God was not personal but through the agency of the high priest.

Blood had to be offered for the high priest as well as for the people's sins. The high priest was a sinner and as such was denied access. He was allowed to appear before God only when blood was shed for him as it specifically was done on the Day of Atonement (Lev. 16:3, 6, 11). The high priest brought blood, not only for himself but also "for the sins the people had committed in ignorance." There are sins people commit deliberately and willfully, without thought of their position as subject to God and without subsequent repentance. The Day of Atonement is not meant to atone for such sins. However there are sins that are serious enough in themselves, but which people would not commit if they realized at the time just what they were doing. Their ignorance is blameworthy, for it is always possible to listen to the voice of God and turn away from evil. But sinners do not always do this. Yet when they sin this may well be out of character, for they are really the people of God and they repent of their sins. For such sins the Day of Atonement is provided.

The writer proceeds to draw a most important conclusion. The ceremonies of the Day of Atonement teach us about approach to God. The people were outside, even the priests had no access past the Holy Place, and the high priest was allowed to enter the Most Holy Place only after taking the most stringent precautions. In all this the Holy Spirit was at work, showing that the way into the Most Holy Place "had not yet been disclosed" (v. 8). The plan of the tabernacle and particularly the position and the function of the curtain marking off the Most Holy Place were significant. They showed those with eyes to see that there was no open access to God. The tabernacle was a vivid lesson in itself. Strictly speaking this means the tabernacle in the wilderness, but what is said of "the first tabernacle" is just as true of the structures that succeeded it. The temple of Solomon and the temple of Herod both embodied precisely the same symbolism in their arrangement, which was patterned after the tabernacle. The author is making the point that it is only Christ who brings people into the presence of God, and the symbolism that shows the ineffectiveness of any other way is just as true of the temple in Jerusalem as it had been of the tent in the wilderness.

The point is emphasized: "This is an illustration for the present time" (v. 9). The tabernacle arrangement and furnishings illustrate an important spiritual truth. The KJV takes the time reference to be to "the time then present," i.e., the time of the tabernacle, and this is a possible understanding of the Greek. It would signify that the way the tabernacle was set up made it clear that the worship carried on in it consisted of ineffective rites. But the words may also be taken to signify "the time now present," in which case we are to understand that the tabernacle arrangement taught a lesson valid for the time at which the epistle was written. It was as true then as in former days (and it is just as true now) that genuine access to God is not to be obtained by offering "gifts and sacrifices." The offerings made under the old covenant were simply "not able to clear the conscience of the worshiper." Animal sacrifice is merely external and cannot come to grips with the problem posed by the guilty conscience. For that something very different is needed.

The externality is emphasized (v. 10). The Levitical system was external through and through. It was taken up with matters like "food and drink and various ceremonial washings." There were many regulations concerning food (see Lev. 11), and some about drinking (e.g., Lev. 11:32–36). Again, priests must not use alcohol while they carried out their ministry (Lev. 10:8–9) and Nazirites must not use it either (Num. 6:2–3). On the positive side, there were drink offerings made to the Lord (Num. 6:15, 17; 28:7–8, etc.). Ceremonial washings were, of course, a feature of the Levitical religion; they were required for priests during their ministry

(Exod. 30:20–21) and for people who had become "unclean" in some way (Lev. 15:4–27, etc.). Ceremonial purity was important and "washings" were the way to achieve this.

But none of this concerns our inner state. It is all a matter of what the writer calls "external regulations" or "regulations for the body" (RSV; literally, "fleshly" regulations). These things had their place in the old scheme of things, but they applied only "until the time of the new order." The writer does not say what that new order is, but the whole thrust of his argument is that it refers to the new covenant that Christ mediated, a covenant that is concerned with our hearts and minds as was prophesied in Scripture (8:10).

D. The Blood of Christ (9:11–14)

From ineffective rites the writer moves to the effective work of Christ and shows that He saves not from ceremonial defilement but from evil deeds that hurt our consciences and "lead to death" (v. 14). He speaks of Christ as "high priest" (v. 11), carrying on the view of His person that is most suitable when considering the liturgical approach to God. There is a problem whether we should understand Him as a high priest "of the good things that are already here" (NIV, RSV, etc.) or of the "good things to come" (KJV). Some manuscripts have one reading, some the other. A decision is not easy, but the NIV reading seems preferable, partly because of the quality of the manuscripts that have this reading and partly because copyists would be inclined to alter it to "good things to come," whereas they would not be likely to make the reverse alteration. The author then seems to be saying that Christ's work as high priest has produced a new state of affairs. There is much about it yet to be unfolded, but the new age has already been inaugurated.

There is a further problem in the "greater and more perfect tabernacle." Some have understood this to mean Jesus' humanity—Jesus came in human flesh and in this way brought about the "good things." But it seems more likely that we should understand the words to refer to Christ's ministry in heaven in the very presence of God (cf. v. 24). The salvation our Great High Priest secured is a salvation effective in heaven. It was not brought about by any such sacrifices as those offered by the Levitical priests. The author insists that Christ's work was done in the tabernacle "that is not man-made" and "not a part of this creation." While the sacrifice Christ offered took place on a physical cross on a definite day in a definite land on this physical earth, the essence of that sacrifice was that it was effective in the presence of God. It was not simply an earth-bound activity as the Levitical sacrifices were. There was no earthly temple or tabernacle in which Christ offered His sacrifice.

Some versions express the thought that Christ took His blood into heaven (v. 12; cf. JB, "taking with him not the blood of goats and bull calves, but his own blood"). Such translations are not accurate, for the Greek says simply "through the blood" (there is no verb "taking"). And they introduce a theological error that flies in the face of our author's fundamental thought that Christ's death on the cross is the final sacrifice that puts away sin. To introduce the idea that He had to take His blood into heaven and thus continue His saving work there is quite foreign to the author's emphasis on the "once-for-all" nature of the saving work on the cross. Nothing needs to be added to that (and nothing can be added). He entered heaven "through" His own blood. He did not take His blood there to do something that His sacrifice on the cross could not do.

The effectiveness of that sacrifice is further emphasized. The ceremonies of the Day of Atonement seem to lie behind what is said at this point, with the references to "goats and calves," to "the Most Holy Place," and in the next verse to "goats and bulls." It was not through animal blood that Christ made atonement but through His own blood. The superior quality of His sacrifice of Himself is further brought out with the characteristic "once for all." The utter finality of Christ's sacrifice is in mind. Nothing can be added to it and it never needs to be repeated.

By it Christ "obtained eternal redemption." Redemption is a picturesque word, referring originally to the setting free of a prisoner of war by the paying of a ransom price. It was then used of the freeing of a slave by the same process and sometimes of the setting free of someone under sentence of death (e.g., Exod. 21:29–30). It might be used in a similar way of property (e.g., Lev. 25:25), though that is not our specific concern. But however the word was used, the basic idea is that of paying a price to secure freedom. From one point of view that is what the cross means. Sinners are slaves (John 8:34), but Christ paid the price and they are now free. "Eternal" redemption is redemption without end. When Christ sets us free we are free indeed.

Now the writer looks back to the ceremonial cleanness that was all that the old sacrifices could accomplish (v. 13). He draws attention to two specially solemn rites of purification, that on the Day of Atonement ("the blood of goats and bulls") and that brought about by the slaying of the red heifer to provide the "water of cleansing." The heifer was burned and its ashes put in water, and the liquid was used in the ceremonial cleansing of the defiled (see Num. 19). But all that such solemn rites could effect was outward; they made the worshipers "outwardly clean."

The superiority of Christ's offering is brought out with a "how much more" argument (v. 14). "The blood of Christ" points to the death of Christ, as often in the New Testament. This blood does not cleanse simply outwardly; it cleanses "our consciences" and it cleanses "from acts that lead to death." This is on a very different plane from the Levitical sacrifices—it deals with our deepest needs. The result is that we "serve the living God." The redeemed are in communion with God and therefore can render Him the service that is His due.

There is a well-known difficulty in this verse in that it is not clear whether "the eternal Spirit" is to be understood as referring to the Holy Spirit or whether we should understand the term to mean Jesus' own human spirit. Nowhere else is the Holy Spirit called "the eternal Spirit," which leads some to favor the application to Jesus' own spirit. The words would then mean that Jesus' whole nature, including His spirit, was involved in His saving work, or that Jesus offered Himself in His essential nature, which is spirit. But it seems more likely that it is the Holy Spirit that is in mind, even if the description is unusual. After all, the Holy Spirit is eternal, even if this is not said explicitly in other places. What this passage is saying, then, is that the Holy Spirit was involved in the atonement, just as the Father was (e.g., John 3:16). It was "through the eternal Spirit" that Christ offered Himself, a sacrifice that is "unblemished." This word was a technical term in the language of sacrifice and indicated that an animal was without defect and thus fit for sacrifice. Jesus was fully qualified to offer the sacrifice He did.

E. The Mediator of the New Covenant (9:15–22)

The writer proceeds to develop the implications of the death of Jesus and to relate it to the making of the new covenant. Grammatically, "For this reason" may be held to look either backward to the sacrifice Christ offered or forward to the receiving of the inheritance. Both are true, but perhaps here there is more to be said for the backward look: the words carry on the discussion of the death of Jesus. He is now seen as "the mediator of a new covenant," where the term "mediator" is one that may be used of a neutral but interested party who brings together people who were at odds, sometimes with the added thought that he guarantees the settlement that is reached. Jesus is seen as bringing God and man together. Sin had estranged them; the old covenant had been broken. But Jesus mediated the new covenant by His death, a covenant in which those who are called "receive the promised eternal inheritance" (v. 15). Mediatorship implies the divine initiative (sinners did not look for or produce a mediator), which is also reflected in the words "those who are called." It is only as God calls us out of our sins that we enter His salvation. "Promised eternal inheritance" brings before us three concepts of great importance in this epistle. We have already noticed that the writer puts emphasis on the promises of God: all that happened in Christ represented the outworking of what God had promised. His good gift is not for a moment but is "eternal": the readers were tempted to slip back into something that could bring them no more than a temporary respite from trouble and for that they were throwing away that which is eternal. And "inheritance," which strictly means a possession that we receive as the result of the death of its previous owner, is used by this writer to denote something that is securely ours. All three are important for an understanding of what Christ has done for us.

When he speaks of Christ as having "died as a ransom," the writer is using the same picturesque form of speech as he did earlier (v. 12). Christ paid the price and now His people go free. Perhaps we should notice that, while the process of redemption is one that was widely known in antiquity, the New Testament writers use an unusual word for it. It is as if, while appealing to what everyone knew, they want their readers to see that there is something unusual about Christ's redemption. It is not rightly seen as simply another example of what was done commonly. It was distinctive.

The writer makes a most important point when he says that it is the death of Jesus that avails for "the sins committed under the first covenant." The blood of bulls and goats cannot take away sin (10:3). But faithful people in Old Testament times were saved. Why? Because the death of Jesus works backward as well as forward; His death puts away all the sins of all who are redeemed whenever and wherever their lives ran their course.

It is not easy to bring out the force of the next stage of the argument in English because we do not have a word that has the dual meaning of "testament" and "covenant." The writer refers to the new "covenant" Jesus made (v. 15) and he still has this in mind when he goes on to refer to "a will" (v. 16), using the very same Greek word (see comments on 7:22). His point is that what is true of a will is true of the covenant Jesus made. A will does not take effect until the one who made it dies. Obviously, as long as the testator is alive there is always the possibility that the old will may be destroyed and a new one put in its place. But when the testator dies there is no possibility of alteration; his death brings the will into effect. So the death of Jesus brings the new covenant into effect. Death is as necessary in the one case as the other.

Even in the case of the first covenant we can see something like this (v. 18). In the solemn rites with which it was set up there was the shedding of blood and the solemn manipulation of the blood (see Exod. 24:6, 8). Moses gave the law to the people (v. 19) and proceeded to perform certain ritual acts. Interestingly, the writer lists some things that are not mentioned in the account in Exodus 24: water, scarlet wool, hyssop, and the sprinkling of the book. Water, scarlet, and hyssop were used in cleansing rites, such as the cleansing of the healed leper (Lev. 14:4–6; it is not said whether the scarlet was to be of wool or some other material, but wool was common). Hyssop was often linked with cleansing (cf. Ps. 51:7), as was water. The sprinkling of the scroll was possibly done because the scroll was written by sinful men and the defilement they brought to it was thus recognized and taken away.

The climax came in the proclamation of the covenant (v. 20) in words that remind us of those used by Jesus when He instituted the Lord's Supper (Mark 14:24). Both covenants were inaugurated with blood.

In similar fashion, Moses later used blood at the consecration of the tabernacle (another point not mentioned in the Old Testament; but we read about it in the Jewish historian Josephus). Blood was put on Aaron and his sons when they were consecrated as priests, and also on the altar (Exod. 29:20); blood was also put on the altar each year to "make atonement" (Exod. 30:10). While our author's statement that "the tabernacle and everything used in its ceremonies" was sprinkled with blood (v. 21) is more inclusive than the Old Testament record, what he says fits in with all we know; certainly a considerable number of passages speak of cleansing with blood. Indeed, "the law requires that nearly everything be cleansed with blood" (v. 22). There can be no doubt but that the blood of the animal sacrifices loomed large in the old covenant; "nearly everything" required it. Someone who could not afford even small birds for an offering could indeed present a cereal offering (Lev. 5:11–13), and some cleansing was effected with water (Lev. 15:10) and even on exceptional occasions with incense (Num. 16:46) or gold (Num. 31:50). But all these are exceptions. There is no doubt about the rule, and the writer sums up the provisions in the Law with the succinct statement, "without the shedding of blood there is no forgiveness." That is the great lesson taught by the old covenant. Good intentions are not enough. It is the shedding of blood that counts. And the blood that matters is the blood of Christ, as the writer goes on to show.

F. The Perfect Sacrifice (9:23–28)

As he has done before, the writer reasons from what was done under the old covenant in symbol to what is done under the new in fact. He argues that it was "necessary" that what went on in the tabernacle ("the copies") be purified in this way, but "the heavenly things themselves" needed better sacrifices (v. 23). It is not easy to see how heaven needs any kind of sacrifices, but we must remember that the New Testament speaks of "the spiritual forces of evil in the heavenly realms" (Eph. 6:12) and also of God as having reconciled to Himself through Christ "things in heaven" as well as "things on earth" (Col. 1:20). Whatever needed cleansing, whether in earth or heaven, is cleansed only with the blood of Christ, the "better" sacrifice that is truly effective. The plural, "sacrifices," is the generic plural; it lays down the principle and is not to be taken as indicating more than one, for, as the writer makes clear again and again, there is only one sacrifice that can take away sin and that is the one sacrifice of Christ, offered once.

The effectiveness of that sacrifice is brought out by reminding us again that Christ did not minister in some "man-made sanctuary" like the tabernacle, which was no more than "a copy of the true one" (v. 24; cf. 8:1–5). His ministry is exercised in heaven, in the presence of God Himself. Notice that He appears there explicitly "for us"; His sacrifice avails to put away *our* sin.

It goes perhaps without saying that if He is in the presence of God on our behalf, nothing more is needed, but the writer does say it anyway. Clearly it is of the greatest importance that Christ's one sacrifice avails. The point has been made before and is given emphasis here. Readers are reminded of the Aaronic high priest with his annual entrance into the Most Holy Place. The Day of Atonement ceremonies bring out the point. On that day and on that day alone, the high priest could enter the Most Holy Place. He must do so with due care, "with blood that is not his own" (v. 25). He could not enter without blood and the blood could not possibly be his own, for if it were he would be dead. His entrance was a symbol of something more, and the writer says explicitly that Christ did not enter heaven "again and again" on the model of the earthly high priest. Had that been the case He would have had to suffer "many times" (v. 26): He would have had to become incarnate again and again and die over and over.

But to see atonement as brought about in this way is to miss the central point, which is that Christ has appeared "once for all." That is the point about His sacrifice our author keeps hammering at. We are not to think of a multiplicity of sacrifices for sin. That would be a complete misunderstanding. When Christ sacrificed Himself He did away with sin. Sin is finished by that sacrifice. A repetition is unthinkable. Christ appeared "at the end of the ages," which some take to mean the author thought that he was living in the last days. If we understand it in this way, we should see that the coming of Christ has made all things new; it ushered in the final state of things. But more probably we should think of a meaning like "the climax of history" (NEB). Christ's atonement is the watershed. It divides all history into B.C. and A.D. It is the central happening on which all else pivots.

From yet another point of view the uniqueness of Christ's sacrifice is emphasized. People die once and there is a finality about it (v. 27). The word translated "once for all," which we have seen applied to Christ's sacrifice (v. 26), is now applied to the death of man. It is final, the complete end to earthly life. But it is not the final end, for it is followed by judgment. The writer does not say when that judgment will be; it is enough that it is certain. Many people, then as now, saw death as the end of everything; they did not see themselves as accountable to God. The writer does not dwell on judgment or draw out its implications. The main thrust of his argument concerns what Christ has done. But he is clear that judgment is a reality for all who die.

Just as people die once, so did Christ die once, but with the important difference that His death was a sacrifice that takes away people's sins. The expression translated "to take away the sins" more literally means "to bear sins"; this is one of only two places in the New Testament where Christ is said to bear sins (the other is 1 Peter 2:24). The idea is frequent in the Old Testament, where it is clear that bearing sin means bearing the penalty of sin (see Num. 14:34; Ezek. 18:20; in both passages the original means "bear sin"; cf. KJV). In these two New Testament passages there may be a recollection of the Suffering Servant who is twice said to bear sin (Isa. 53:11, 12). The writer is saying that Christ suffered the penalty of sin that sinners had deserved.

He adds a reference to the Second Coming. It will not be to deal with sin, for that has been done already. Rather, it will be "to bring salvation." There is a sense in which salvation has been won: nothing can be added to the perfection of Christ's atonement, a truth on which the author insists many times. But the saved do not enter into all that salvation means until Christ's return and in that sense salvation is future. Believers are described as "those who are waiting for him": they look eagerly for His return (cf. Titus 2:13; 2 Peter 3:12, etc.)

For Further Study

1. What is the meaning of "covenant"? Make a list of the characteristics of the old covenant and those of the new.
2. What can we learn about the salvation Christ brings from the quotation from Jeremiah 31 in Hebrews 8:8–12?
3. Look up "tabernacle" in a Bible dictionary or encyclopedia. What lessons can the Christian learn from the way the tabernacle was set up?
4. What passages can you find that speak of the work of Christ as redemption? What do they tell us about our salvation?
5. List all the ways in which the writer brings out the finality of Christ's death for sinners.

Chapter 8

A New and Better Covenant (II)

(Hebrews 10:1–39)

It is central to the writer's thinking that the Jewish way is ineffective. The animal sacrifices can never take away sin, though they do remind us that sin is serious and that it is taken away only by the shedding of blood. Now he brings out the thought that the sacrifice Jesus made was of a different order. It was not the offering of some poor dumb beast, uncomprehending and unwilling, but the offering of a will perfectly yielded to the doing of the Father's will. That sacrifice has consequences.

A. The Law a Shadow (10:1–4)

"The law" (v. 1) here stands for the whole Old Testament system, though strictly it means "the law of Moses" (the books Genesis through Deuteronomy). The Old Testament system was not the reality the readers were being led to suppose. It was no more than "a shadow," something unreal as opposed to that which has substance. At the same time, a shadow is related to that of which it is a shadow. From the Old Testament shadow something may be deduced about the reality, but at this point the argument concentrates on the fact that it is no more than a shadow. Because of its essential nature it cannot *do* things; specifically, it cannot "make perfect those who draw near to worship." The point receiving emphasis is the continual repetition of the sacrifices. That they are offered "year after year" shows that the annual Day of Atonement ceremonies are primarily in mind. If these sacrifices had succeeded in doing what the worshipers hoped for, they would no longer have been offered (v. 2); there is no point in continuing to offer animals when the aim has been achieved. The very continuation of the sacrifices is a standing witness to their ineffectiveness.

Now come three statements about what the animal sacrifices could not do, the implication in each case being that Christ has done it. The first is that the sacrifices cannot "make perfect those who draw near to worship" (v. 1). It is not unlikely that, instead of "repeated endlessly," we should understand the words as "bring the worshippers to perfection for all time" (NEB). The animal sacrifices could not bring about the permanent perfection of the worshipers. The second point is like the first. If those sacrifices had been effective, "the worshipers would have been cleansed once for all" (v. 2; "once for all" is the term used so often of the sacrifice of Christ). Thirdly, they would "no longer have felt guilty for their sins," though "felt guilty" does not sufficiently bring out the meaning of the Greek, which uses the word "conscience": "the conscience would have been cleansed" (cf. 9:9, 14; 10:22).

These things the animal sacrifices do not accomplish. What then do they do? They remind the worshipers of sins (v. 3). They do not let us forget that sin is a barrier to fellowship with God and that something must be done if that barrier is to be removed. But they themselves do not remove it. The author roundly declares that "it is impossible" for animal blood to deal with human sin (v. 4). The limitations of the Levitical system are imposed by the fact that the best sacrifices it could produce were those of animals, which stand on a lower plane than people.

B. One Sacrifice for Sins (10:5–18)

While he has had Scripture in mind through much of chapter 9, the writer has not actually quoted it very much. But he has the habit of driving home his points by quoting from his Bible and he does that now. He reminds his readers of Psalm 40:6–8, which stresses the importance of doing the will of God, and sets this over against the sacrifices. Interestingly, he sees the psalm as the utterance of Christ (the word "Christ" is not in the Greek text of verse 5 but is clearly implied), spoken at the threshhold of the Incarnation and thus expressing something of the purpose of Christ's coming into the world.

The writer speaks of "sacrifice," "offering," "burnt offerings," and "sin offerings." These are not the only sacrifices in the Levitical system, but they may be taken as a comprehensive overview. Together they indicate something of the variety of the offerings in the sacrificial system and also of the ineffectiveness of the whole. The words "you did not desire" and "you were not pleased" should not be taken to indicate that the sacrificial system was contrary to the will of God. It was set up by God's command and it teaches important spiritual lessons (e.g., v. 3). Wherever the sacrifices were the expression of genuine penitence and a sincere desire to do the will of God they were acceptable. But sacrifice, regarded simply as the offering of an animal, an external victim, in place of the worshiper, the kind of sacrifice that was all too common in the psalmist's day, was not the will of God. God took no delight in the routine performance of the ritual of sacrifice.

The writer quotes from the Septuagint, which has "a body you prepared for me," whereas the Hebrew text has literally "ears you have dug for me." The Septuagint translators presumably regarded the hollowing out of the ears as part of the making of the body and they took the part for the whole. By his reference to the ear the psalmist probably had in mind that it is this organ by which we hear the voice of God and which can lead us to obedience. The thrust of the passage is that obedience is more important than sacrifice (cf. "To obey is better than sacrifice, and to heed is better than the fat of rams"; 1 Sam. 15:22).

All this leads up to the thought that the speaker has come to do the will of God (v. 7). In the ritual performance of the act of sacrifice the uncomprehending animals were not and could not be consulted as to what they wanted to do in the matter. But in the case of Christ, the final sacrifice, the will was involved: Christ says that He has come to do the will of God. The will of the Son is perfectly aligned with the will of the Father.

The point is further clarified in verse 8. The writer quotes again the words about God's not desiring animal sacrifice and adds that this is so even though such sacrifices are required in the Law. But, of course, the Law envisages sacrifices offered in the right spirit, while the epistle refers to animal sacrifice as the external act of killing animals and performing the prescribed actions. External ritualism does not meet the requirements of a holy God. The worshiper who merely goes through the motions cannot defend himself by saying, "I am doing what the Law commands." The psalm makes it clear that it is not that kind of offering that is pleasing to God.

Having drawn attention a second time to what the psalm says about the sacrifices, our author goes on to the words, "Here I am, I have come to do your will" (v. 9). It is the will that matters. Without the yielded will the sacrifices do not matter. The writer goes so far as to say, "He sets aside the first to establish the second." He does not define his "first" or "second," but there is no doubt that he is contrasting Judaism with the Christian way. The place of the will in the offering of sacrifice is so important that it invalidates the former and establishes the latter. The sacrifice of unwilling, uncomprehending animals has been set aside. The sacrifice that involves the yielded will of Christ is effectual.

But we must be on our guard against thinking that it is only the will that is important. Some writers have given the impression that what happened on Calvary was important only in the sense that Jesus was perfectly ready to do the will of God. They suggest that the only thing involved in the sacrifice was His yielded will. But the New Testament continually refers to the blood of Christ being shed, to the cross, to His death, and so forth. This passage makes it clear that in the providence of God the offering of "the body" was significant. There is emphasis on the importance of the will, but we should not reason as though the writer meant that when Jesus said "not my will, but yours be done" (Luke 22:42) the atonement was effected. Granted that without that agreement of will nothing would have been accomplished, it is yet the case that the will in question was that "the body of Jesus Christ" be offered in sacrifice.

Characteristically, the writer adds that Jesus' sacrifice was "once for all." It is fundamental to him that there was one sacrifice once offered. And it is this that makes us holy, i.e., enables us to be God's own people, set apart for Him. No other sacrifice than the sacrifice of Christ can do this.

The "once for all" leads to a comparison with the Levitical priests (v. 11). Every such priest is at work "day after day." Where Christ offered His sacrifice at one moment in time, the Levitical priests must work at it day after day. "Again and again" every such priest offers his sacrifices. It is pathetic because the sacrifices can never deal with sins. The uniqueness of Christ's sacrifice is stressed with the reminder that it was "for all time" and that it was "one sacrifice for sins" (v. 12). There is also a contrast in posture: each Levitical priest "stands," whereas Christ "sat down." No priest was permitted to sit during the time of his ministration; it is specifically said that he is "to stand and minister in the Lord's name" (Deut. 18:5). This posture symbolized an ongoing work; it was never done. But Christ accomplished His work and "sat down." His posture indicates a completed work, a work done once and for all that does not need repetition. As before, the writer adds that Christ is at God's right hand, the place of highest honor in heaven. This contrasts with the suppliant attitude of the priests. We should perhaps notice that even angels do not sit, but stand before God (Luke 1:19). It is no small claim the writer makes about Jesus. We see something of the way this claim was regarded in that, when Jesus claimed that He would sit at God's right hand and come in the clouds of heaven, the high priest saw this as such serious blasphemy that he tore his robes (Mark 14:62–63).

The writer has another interesting picture of Jesus' activity when he says that He now "waits for his enemies to be made his footstool" (v. 13; the words are an adaptation of Ps. 110:1). The enemies are not defined, but we should understand them to be everything that is evil. There is a sense in which the victory has already been secured, for Christ's death has defeated the foe (Col. 2:15). But there is another sense in which, though the decisive battle has been fought and won, the consummation of the victory is yet future. It will await the return of Christ (1 Cor. 15:23–26). This is what is in mind here: the saving work is done, but evil still is at work in the world. In the end it will be completely abolished, as the making of the enemies into a footstool so powerfully depicts.

The writer rounds off this section of the argument by citing the one sacrifice as the reason for Christ's waiting (v. 14). There is nothing more for Christ to do because His sacrifice has perfected His people forever. Notice yet once more the reference to "one sacrifice" and to "forever." The uniqueness and the perfection of Christ's saving work are before our writer continually. The saved are "made perfect forever," which is the thought we have already seen a number of times that they are perfectly fit to stand before God and that this is lasting. They are also "those who are being made holy." Some have understood this to refer to the continuing process of sanctification, which is such a prominent feature of Paul's teaching. This is possible but unlikely, since the writer does not give attention to this aspect of the Christian life in his epistle. It is more probable that it is a timeless present with the meaning, "he has made perfect the people he sets apart to be God's." Or the reference may be to the continuing process of bringing people out of the darkness of sin into the light of the gospel, or perhaps more specifically to those who at the time of writing were being brought into salvation. Whatever view we take of this in detail, the thrust of the argument is clear: Christ's one sacrifice of Himself forever perfects the people He sanctifies.

Now comes an appeal to Scripture. Notice that "The Holy Spirit" is the author of Scripture (cf. 3:7). Consistently the writer looks beyond the human authors to the God who inspired them, though it is not often that he refers to the Spirit. But he always regards his Bible as coming from God. He has already quoted from Jeremiah 31:31–34 at length (8:8–12). Now he refers again to the same passage but shortens it considerably. We get an interesting insight into his thinking by noticing the parts of Jeremiah 31 on which he concentrates. He quotes the words about God making the covenant and about His writing His laws within the people, on their hearts and minds. He omits everything else until he comes to the words about forgiveness: this is what matters. The new covenant, for our writer, is a covenant that is inward and brings real forgiveness, not simply a reminder of sins, which was the best the old way could do (v. 3).

Having cited the passage from Jeremiah, the writer draws a conclusion that does not seem to have occurred to his contemporary Jewish friends. If sins are really forgiven "there is no longer any sacrifice for sin" (v. 18). Where can there possibly be a place for a sacrifice to put away sin when sin has been done away completely? The fulfillment of the prophecy means the complete abandonment of the way the Jews valued so highly.

C. The Sequel—The Right Way (10:19–25)

The writer has completed the exposition of Jesus' saving work that is at the heart of the epistle. But the readers must not think that, because the one sacrifice that has been offered has perfectly done away with sins, nothing else matters. They must not simply relax, saying in effect, "Since Christ has suffered, it does not matter what we do (or don't do!)." On the contrary. What Christ has done indicates the seriousness with which God takes the problem of saving sinful people. Sinners cannot well ignore the implications of the costly sacrifice Christ has offered for them. In order, the author deals with the right response and the wrong one to all this.

The right response begins with confidence (v. 19); "Therefore" relates this confidence to the preceding. It is not a facile, human ignoring of difficulties or an unthinking attitude of "I'm all right, Jack." It is the consequence of a careful, trustful consideration of what Christ has done. If we understand the meaning of the one sacrifice once offered, we have a confidence that nothing else can give us, a confidence not concerned with some minor matter of earthly things but with entering the presence of God. The "Most Holy Place" and the reference to blood show that the Day of Atonement ceremonies are in the writer's mind. On that one day in all the year there was access into the Most Holy Place that symbolized the presence of God. We usually think of the Day of Atonement as a day in which there was a solemn remembrance of sins and an impressive ritual for forgiveness. But in Leviticus the observance of the day is introduced with the words, "Tell your brother Aaron not to come whenever he chooses into the Most Holy Place. . . . This is how Aaron is to enter the sanctuary area . . ." (Lev. 16:2–3). Access into the presence of God was jealously guarded. The best that the old way could offer was a symbolic entrance and that on just one day in the year and after adequate precautions had been taken.

But Christ's sacrifice means that "a new and living way" has been opened up (v. 20). More literally, the way has been "dedicated"; the same word is used of the dedication of the first covenant in 9:18 (where it is translated "put into effect"). The old way was dedicated with blood and this new way was dedicated with blood. The curtain reminds us of the curtain that separated the Most Holy Place from the rest of the tabernacle. The presence of God lay symbolically on the other side of that curtain, but that curtain was torn in two at the time of the death of Jesus (Matt. 27:51; Mark 15:38; Luke 23:45). In recording this, the gospel writers bring out the truth that the way into the presence of God was opened up by the death of Jesus; our author is making the same point in his own way. He tells us that "the curtain" is Christ's body. We do not usually reason like this, for we think of the Incarnation (Christ's being in the body) as the way God revealed Himself to us, not as a concealment. But no one will say that the body of Christ perfectly reveals God. The hymn writer has expressed this truth in the words, "Veiled in flesh the Godhead see." Jesus is God's revelation to us, but there is much more about God than we see in the Incarnation.

The great truth set forth here is that it was "through" the curtain, the body (more strictly, "flesh") of Jesus that the way to God was made open. The curtain was torn; the body was broken on the cross; the way to God was opened wide.

With this is linked the thought that we have "a great priest over the house of God" (v. 21). We generally speak of a "high" priest, but the Hebrew expression more literally means "great" priest; we have here thus a literal rendering that at the same time draws attention to Christ's greatness, since this is a very unusual way to refer to a high priest in Greek (or for that matter, in English). We have previously seen that Christ is a Son over God's household (3:6); here we have that thought combined with the other idea that He exercises important priestly functions. He is both priest and Son and He is over God's people in both capacities.

We come to an impressive series of exhortations. Since Christ has opened up the way, and since He is such a great priest, we should "draw near to God" (v. 22). That cannot be done by the Jewish manner of approach. In the tabernacle (and the temple) the Most Holy Place was screened off and only the high priest might approach and he only once a year. But now that the way into the holiest has been opened, it is imperative that we use it. To ignore the way that Christ has opened up by His death is disaster.

Entrance is to be made "with a sincere heart." The heart stands for the whole of the inner state of man, so this is a way of saying that the real approach to God is not in externals. It depends on being right in one's innermost being. The expression rendered here "with a sincere heart" is the same as "with a perfect heart," used of Hezekiah's walk with God (Isa. 38:3; see KJV). There is a reference to "having our hearts sprinkled," which, in view of the reference to the washing of the body with water, probably refers to Christian baptism. It brings out an important truth in a day when all religions had washings of one kind or another, which were all too often taken as ritual requirements and no more. Christian baptism includes an external washing, but the more important aspect is that it is simply an outward sign of an inner cleansing without which it is meaningless. The writer reminds the readers of their baptism and invites them to reflect on its meaning: it points to that inward cleansing that deals with a guilty conscience. This approach to God is linked with "full assurance of faith," which brings out the truth that it is only as we rely on Christ that this inward cleansing and this approach to God can take place.

The second exhortation is that we retain "unswervingly" the hope we profess as Christians (v. 23). The writer has already said that we are God's household if we hold to our courage "and the hope of which we boast" (3:6). Hope is one of the distinguishing marks of Christians. We say, "While there's life there's hope." But conversely, when there is no hope, then there is no life worth the name. Our author is saying that hope is central to the Christian way. Christ takes people who are lost, helpless, aimless, and to them He gives a living hope, a hope that will be an anchor for their souls (6:19). This is a precious possession, enriching all their lives. It is not to be taken lightly, as though it were of no consequence, but to be held unswervingly. The reason for our hope? "He who promised is faithful." That is always the basis. Christians do not retain hope out of naturally sunny dispositions, nor as a facile optimism that pays scant regard to the facts. They retain their hope because it is securely based. It rests on One who is inherently reliable; again and again we are told that He is faithful (cf. 1 Cor. 1:9; 10:13; 1 Thess. 5:24; 2 Thess. 3:3; 2 Tim. 2:13; 1 John 1:9, etc.). It is the faithfulness of God that gives Christians a hope that is unshakeable.

The third exhortation concerns love (v. 24). Notice that in these three verses we have faith, hope, and love linked, as often in the New Testament. Clearly the early Christians saw the trio as very important and as summing up much of the Christian way. Love, as the Christians understood it, is not the surrender to selfish passion (as it is so often understood today), nor is it the kindness that worldly people readily show to one another (Luke 6:32). We find out what love means when we see the cross (Rom. 5:8; 1 John 4:10). It is a love that proceeds from the fact that God is love (1 John 4:8, 16). God loves quite irrespective of human merit. He loves because it is His nature to love, because He is a loving God. Christians are to love like He does (John 15:12; 1 John 4:11). Transformed by the love of God at work in them they begin to love because they have at least in some measure become loving people. They love because they have been loved (1 John 4:19). The fruit of the Spirit within them is love (Gal. 5:22). Love is costly. But there is no substitute for it in Christian salvation or in Christian service. Love issues in good deeds, for it is intensely practical (1 John 3:17–18). So now the writer urges his friends to be active in loving works. In this world people are often apt to be provocative, but the only provocation to which believers should give way is the spurring of one another on to deeds of love. There is no way of emphasizing this too strongly.

As the NIV renders it, we appear to have a fourth exhortation, "Let us not give up meeting together" (v. 25), but in fact this is part of the preceding, the verb being a participle so that the passage means, "Let us consider how we may spur one another on toward love . . . not forsaking meeting together. . . ." The point is that loving people meet together. Love does not leave other Christians to get on as best they can but meets with them to help where that is possible. The regular gathering of Christians has always been important and it must have been especially important in the first century. As Moffatt puts it, "Any early Christian who attempted to live like a pious particle without the support of the community ran serious risks in an age when there was no public opinion to support him." The Christian is a member of the redeemed community, not "a pious particle." If I try to live like a "pious particle" I impoverish myself and I fail to act in love toward others in the Christian fellowship. We need one another in the Christian life.

The writer gives no indication of who were forsaking the Christian meeting or of why they did this. It is enough that there were such people, and their example is to be avoided. They possibly saw Christianity as just another of the religions in the Roman world of their day. They could take it or leave it, attend its worship or stay away just as it pleased them. But this was to miss the point that was central to the author's thinking—Christ is God's final word to men. Once that truth is accepted it is impossible to put Christianity on a level with the other religions of antiquity. The assembling of Christians is not to be seen as a pleasant social activity in which believers may indulge or not, according to taste. It is part of their response to God's unique act in sending His Son to be their Savior.

On the contrary, believers are to "encourage one another," and their meeting together is a means of encouragement. The point is that Christians are concerned for one another and realize their weakness; we all need all the help we can get and the encouragement of fellow believers is an important part of this. The writer enforces this by referring to the approach of what he calls simply "the Day." This is probably to be thought of as the Day of Judgment, the day when Christ will return. Some have confidently claimed that the reference is to the fall of Jerusalem; they see the letter as written during the war between the Jews and the Romans and think that it is its climax that is in view. This is possible, but it is much more likely that it is Christ's return that is in mind. There is nothing in the whole letter to suggest that the fall of Jerusalem was in the minds of writer and readers.

D. The Sequel—The Wrong Way (10:26–31)

The writer has outlined the response for which he is looking in his correspondents. Now he reinforces his words by drawing their attention to the catastrophic consequences of reacting in the wrong way to what Christ has done. Judgment is real and it is serious. If people reject the love of God they are left to face the judgment of God. Notice his use of "we." He is not adopting a position of superiority, talking down to his readers; he is classing himself with them. The danger of which he writes faces him as well as them. He speaks of "deliberately" continuing in sin, which means much more than an occasional lapse from faithful Christian practice. It means habitual activity, and moreover, habitual activity deliberately chosen "after we have received the knowledge of the truth" (v. 26). The writer is not referring to sins done in ignorance. "The truth" here is the truth of the Christian way, the truth about Christ. When people come to know what Christ has done for them in dying on the cross, when they know that they are called to believe and to live lives of trust and love, then they should act on their knowledge. If they reject it, "no sacrifice for sins is left." They cannot plead ignorance. They have come to know the right way and have turned from it. Now they can expect only judgment and they wait in "fearful expectation" (v. 27). The word translated "fearful" is an unusual one, found elsewhere in the New Testament only in verse 31 and 12:21; it means that the fiery judgment that finally awaits the enemies of God (cf. Isa. 26:11) is nothing less than "frightening."

This is reinforced with a "how much more" argument based on the known seriousness of rejecting the law of Moses. For Jews that law was divinely given; it was the summit of God's revelation and must be obeyed to the letter. There is a particularly relevant passage that refers to people who violated the covenant with God and turned to other gods—such people are to be put to death. There must be "two or three witnesses" (nobody is to be executed simply because someone else says he should), but when that testimony is available the law must take its course (Deut. 17:2–7).

If it is bad to despise Moses' law, it is infinitely worse to despise the new covenant that Christ has made in His blood. To turn away from the old revelation was disastrous; how much worse to turn away from that revelation that involves the Son of God and cost that Son His life!

Three things are especially singled out in the unbelieving rejection of Christ. The person who does this "has trampled the Son of God under foot" (v. 29). This is a strong expression and an unusual use of the verb. Wherever it is used in other New Testament passages it refers to treading on physical objects; this is the only place where a person is the object of the verb. It is a vivid way of bringing out what is involved in rejecting Christ. We get something of its force in the passage referring to giving pearls to pigs who, realizing nothing of their great worth, "may trample them under their feet" (Matt. 7:6). To trample Christ under foot is to scorn Him, to see Him as having no value.

Second, to reject Christ is to despise "the blood of the covenant" (cf. Exod. 24:8; Heb. 9:20 for the use of this expression of the old covenant, and Matt. 26:28; Mark 14:24 of the new). The person who turns away from Christ is treating the blood that Christ shed when He died to inaugurate the new covenant as "unholy" or common. Such a person sees the death of Jesus as no more than the death of anyone else. It may even be worse than most deaths because it was the death of a criminal. To see it as no more than this is a profanation of what is holy and a provocation of the God who sent His Son. That blood "sanctified" the sinner, set him apart to belong to God. It is a serious sin to deny all this.

The third point is that the Christ-rejecting sinner "has insulted the Spirit of grace." In this epistle the emphasis is on what the Father has done through the Son. There is not a great deal about the Holy Spirit, but a passage such as this shows that the writer fully recognized the place of the Spirit in the Godhead and in the giving of the grace of God. He saw the Spirit as a person, for one cannot insult a thing. Nowhere else is the Spirit called "the Spirit of grace" (but cf. Zech. 12:10). He is both the gift of grace and the source of grace. There is a strong antithesis between "insulted" and "grace." The former word has the connotation of an insolent self-sufficiency, the latter that of humble dependence on God.

All this is serious because of the certainty of divine judgment (v. 30). The writer appeals to what is common knowledge ("we know") and proceeds to cite a couple of relevant passages of Scripture. The first, from Deuteronomy 32:35 (cf. Rom. 12:19), states that it is the prerogative of God to punish. There are magistrates and judges who administer the affairs of men, but in the end it is God with whom we have to do. "I will repay" rings with the note of certainty, as does the second quotation, "The LORD will judge his people" (Deut. 32:36; Ps. 135:14). The word "judge" may mean "to give a favorable judgment" and thus "deliver" or "vindicate," and it is used of God's intervention on behalf of His people. But when God intervenes it is with an even-handed justice, and if people are rebellious, selfish, and sinful they cannot expect anything but severe punishment. So the writer goes on to say that it is a frightening thing "to fall into the hands of the living God" (v. 31). The word translated "dreadful" is the same one as that rendered "fearful" in verse 27. The sinner should be "frightened" at the prospect. There is, of course, the possibility of being glad at being in the hands of God, as David was. He deliberately chose to fall into the hands of God rather than into those of men (2 Sam. 24:14; 1 Chron. 21:13). But that was a trustful surrender to the mercies of a loving God. It proceeded from faith, not defiance. The writer is here referring to the insolent sinner who rejects the mercy and the grace of God. For such a person, to fall into the hands of the living God is the ultimate disaster.

E. Choose the Right Way (10:32–39)

In an earlier section of the epistle the writer has given a stern warning against falling away from Christ (6:4–8) and he immediately followed it with an expression of confidence in his readers: they will not do that (6:9–12). He does something similar here. Nothing could be more serious than the warning he has just given (vv. 26–31), but he does not give the warning as one who stands in an agony of doubt, fearful every moment that his friends will slip into this most serious of sins. He is confident that they will surely go on with Christ.

He reminds them of what had happened in their early days as Christians (v. 32). They had "received the light," which means that they had emerged from their previous darkness into the light Christ brings (cf. John 8:12). But in those early days as Christians their way had not been easy. They had endured "a great contest"; the word "contest" (*athlēsis*, from which we get our word "athletics") points to vigorous opposition. The term was often used in the early church to denote Christians as spiritual athletes. They were not content with the minimum in Christian service, but put forth their best effort as they strove to defeat sin. The readers had been tested in some great contest with sufferings and they had endured. The writer reminds them of a splendid achievement.

He goes into further detail. "Sometimes" might be understood as "Some of you." In other words, it is not completely certain whether the writer is referring to the same people (with different things happening to them at different times) or to different groups (some of whom had one experience, some the other). Either way he is clear that they had put up with a lot. They had been made a spectacle; they had been publicly insulted and persecuted. Inevitably commentators have speculated on what persecution is in mind. It is not easy to identify it, for most of the expressions describing it are quite general and could refer to any persecution. We find in 12:4 that none of them had yet been killed, which rules out any persecution in Palestine, where James was executed at an early date (Acts 12:2). It also rules out Rome after the Neronian persecution. But any attempt to identify the persecution is hazardous; we simply do not have the information. What matters is that there had been trouble and that the readers had stood firm.

In addition to suffering, there had been the uncomfortable experience of being included with those who were subject to sufferings. And they had made common cause with prisoners (v. 34). In those days prisoners had a very hard time, for little was done for them by the authorities. People were put in prison to be punished—why then make life easy for them? They often lacked even necessary food and depended on their friends to keep them supplied. It is in the context of this situation that our Lord commended those who visited prisoners (Matt. 25:36). But there was, of course, a risk involved in helping those in jail because the authorities were inclined to lump the friends of prisoners with the prisoners. There was no automatic arrest, but there was certainly danger. The readers had gone right ahead.

They had moreover suffered the loss of their goods. "Confiscation" sounds like an official act, but the Greek term often means something like "plundering," which does not suggest the orderly work of officials. But there was plenty of room for minor officials (who were in close touch with the public) to misuse their office for personal gain, and some may have used their opportunities to confiscate the possessions of a hated and misunderstood minority. Or the term may refer to the result of mob violence. Either is possible.

It is fascinating to notice that the believers did not simply put up with this but accepted it "joyfully." They did not let their possessions tyrannize them. When they lost them they rejoiced, for they were the people of God and they had a better possession than any earthly goods. It is always a real source of encouragement to Christians that no one can ever rob them of their riches in Christ. Their possession is both "better" and "lasting." An interesting possibility arises from an ambiguity in the Greek: the words might also be taken in the sense "you had yourselves as a better and lasting possession." This would give a meaning like that of Luke 21:19: "By standing firm you will save yourselves." Either way, the possession (despite NIV, the word is singular) is real, lasting, and of ultimate significance.

The experience of the readers must give confidence (v. 35). That they had suffered so much and so cheerfully shows that they had an understanding of the importance of belonging to Christ. Their values were the right ones. They had been ready to put up with hardship for Christ's sake. Now they are urged not to throw all this away. They have a well-based confidence; let them not give it up. The writer reminds them that there is a reward before them. This is never the basic motive for Christian service, but it is a reality and should not be overlooked.

As he has done a number of times before, the writer calls for perseverance (v. 36). Good intentions and even a good beginning are not enough. The saints of God are those who persevere to the end. Notice the word "need." The writer is referring, not to something optional, which Christians might do or not do as they choose, but to something basic. Christian service is the doing of the will of God, a subject that has come before us earlier in this chapter. Christ came to do the will of God (vv. 7, 9–10)—indeed, it is only because He did this that there are Christians at all. And while our service is on a much smaller scale, doing the will of God is what it is all about. It is the way to receiving what God has promised. The rebellious and the self-willed cut themselves off from the good gifts God has promised His people.

The readers are encouraged with the thought that Christ will come again and that their difficulties will not last forever. The writer speaks of "just a very little while" (v. 37; cf. Isa. 26:20); for the sake of enduring through just a short time the readers should not let themselves be robbed of the reward of which they have just been reminded. Then the author goes on to a quotation from Habakkuk 2:3–4, a passage Paul also cites (Rom. 1:17; Gal. 3:11). There are some small differences between the Hebrew text and the Greek translation, and as he commonly does, our author follows the Greek. The Hebrew speaks of the vision or revelation, and says that it will certainly come, but the Greek translation refers to a person, rather than a vision. Our author has the definite article before "coming one" (which is not found in our texts of the Septuagint). He is making it clear that the passage refers not merely to "a" but to "the" coming One, i.e., the Messiah. This exact expression is used elsewhere to denote the Messiah (e.g., Matt. 11:3; 21:9; John 11:27). Nor was this only a Christian understanding; the rabbis sometimes understood the text in precisely the same way (and used it as a warning against trying to work out the date when the Messiah would come). The first thing about the quotation then is that it assures the readers that there will be no undue delay in the coming of the Messiah bringing out the truth that Jesus Christ, the

Messiah, will come back in God's own time. The fact is certain, though the time is not known. God's people ("my righteous one") must live by faith, i.e., wait patiently and believingly for the Second Coming which will deliver them from their difficulties. But to "shrink back" is to deny God's oversight of the process. God will not be pleased with such a person. The readers are warned from Scripture not to go back on their allegiance to Christ.[1]

As he has done before, the writer expresses his confidence in his readers. He warns them, but he is confident that they will respond. His "But we" (v. 39) does two things: it sets them in contrast with those who shrink back and it links the writer and the reader. His "we" is emphatic; whatever be the case with others, he and they do not belong to the number of the cowardly who shrink back. That way ends in destruction. But writer and readers belong together in the number of those who are "of faith" (he uses the noun, not the verb as does the NIV) and who save their souls.

For Further Study

1. How does the writer bring out the failure of the sacrificial system in this chapter?
2. Make a list of the passages in this epistle that bring out the finality of what Christ has done.
3. What specific things should Christians be doing in response to what God has done for them in Christ?
4. In what ways had the recipients of the epistle suffered for their faith? How do Christians suffer for it today? How does the writer encourage all believers to persevere?
5. What points does the writer make in warning against going back from following Christ?

---

[1]Our author makes another point by reversing the order of the clauses in the rest of his question, so that the words about shrinking back come last. In the Hebrew the words mean that the destruction of the enemy is certain but will take place in God's good time. "The righteous" must wait patiently for God's deliverance—he is to "live by his faith." But to the translators into Greek the text appeared to refer to the coming of the Deliverer: if someone were to appear on the scene and then draw back, he would not be God's Deliverer, God's Messiah.

Chapter 9

Faith

(Hebrews 11:1–40)

The quotation from Habakkuk has introduced us to the thought of faith, and the writer proceeds to develop the theme in the most sustained treatment of the subject in the New Testament. He has his own way of doing this. We should notice two important differences from the way Paul speaks of faith. This writer concentrates on faith in God, whereas Paul so often refers to faith in Christ. And where Paul frequently relates faith to the past, to what God has done in Christ to bring us salvation, this writer relates it to the future: he thinks of the trustful attitude that sustains the believer as he presses on despite difficulties. We should perhaps notice also that Paul sometimes contrasts faith and works, but that this is not in our author's mind at this point. He is concerned rather with sustaining faith, the faith that sees the people of God through all their difficulties. His treatment is a classic. It has brought enlightenment and help to every generation of the Christian church.

A. The Meaning of Faith (11:1–3)

First we have some preliminary remarks on the general nature of faith. These should not be understood as a formal definition but rather as showing some of the basic characteristics of faith. The opening expression is not an easy one and has been translated in a variety of ways. The writer uses the word *hypostasis*, which literally means "a standing under"; it is used of that which underlies the surface appearance, that which makes a thing what it is. Faith is that which "stands under" our hopes. What we hope for is not present with us now, but that does not mean that we may not be certain about it. Christians are certain, for example, of their eternal salvation, though they do not yet see it in all its fullness. What gives certainty is faith. It is all we have at present and it is all we need. It undergirds the Christian life.

There is a different piece of imagery in the second part of verse 1, where we have a word that has a meaning like "proof" or "test." The NIV takes the former meaning and understands the writer to be repeating in another way what he has already said. The whole verse is then saying that it is faith that gives us certainty and assurance. This may well be right. But it is also possible that we should take the term to mean "test." There are unseen realities for which we have no material evidence. We cannot test them out by ordinary human methods of testing, but the Christian has faith, and faith tests all things. What does not accord with faith is to be rejected. This is far-reaching, for "what we do not see" covers the whole range of nonmaterial phenomena. Faith gives certainty and stability over a wide range of the nonmaterial where the unbeliever has nothing to help him.

Faithful men of old ("the ancients") had witness borne to them because they believed. They had great achievements to their credit, but the writer sticks to just one thing, their faith. It is this that makes this chapter so distinctive. There are examples in ancient writings of the commemoration of heroes of the past, perhaps the best-known being the passage in Ecclesiasticus 44:1–50:21, which begins, "Let us now praise famous men." All such passages see a variety of reasons for praising the great, but throughout this chapter there is just one thing—their faith. In the last resort nothing else matters.

But before he works out his thesis by drawing attention to significant happenings in the lives of the great ones of old, the writer joins his readers and himself in an expression of faith (v. 3). It takes faith to see that it is God who is behind this physical universe. Our understanding of the divine origin of the universe is not the end product of a process of reasoning on the basis of scientific evidence (however impressive such a process may be). To believe that the universe exists does not require faith, nor does the idea that the universe as we know it was made out of something that existed before it. But to believe that it was all called into being by the word of God, as Genesis 1 tells us, that requires faith. It is faith that assures us that there is no material explanation of the things that we see, that the universe does not account for itself. But faith also assures us that it is God's universe.

B. The Faith of the Men Before the Flood (11:4–7)

Now the writer proceeds to his demonstration of the importance of faith in the lives of God's people throughout the ages. He makes his selection from the followers of God and shows that in every one of them there is evidence of faith. He goes back to the very beginning, to the first family, and starts with Abel (v. 4). It was "by faith" that Abel offered a better sacrifice than that of Cain. Christians have often looked for some other reason, one commonly suggested being that he offered the blood of animal sacrifice, whereas Cain brought only cereals. But the Bible never says that this is the reason. There is no indication that it was the material brought to God that was superior. The writer says that it was the attitude of the worshiper that mattered: Abel offered "by faith" and it was that that was the significant difference. Because of this, testimony was borne to him ("he was commended"): God Himself bore testimony (the same verb is translated "spoke well"). It is unusual to read of God as bearing testimony to anyone, so that we are to see Abel's faith as specially significant. And for our author it is still significant. He does not regard the story of Abel as simply a piece of ancient history. Abel has been dead for a long time but "he still speaks." Faith lives.

Enoch (v. 5) was a very important figure in Jewish apocalyptic writings and several books bear his name. Evidently the fact that God "took" him (Gen. 5:24) appealed to the apocalyptists, and they let their imaginations run riot on the wonderful possibilities for a man of whom this was said. In the New Testament he is not a prominent figure, being mentioned elsewhere only in Luke 3:37 and Jude 14. It is not explicitly said in Genesis that he had faith, but the writer points out that this is implied. "Without faith it is impossible to please God" (v. 6), and as Enoch did please Him (he "walked with God," Gen. 5:24), the conclusion is inescapable. In his case faith resulted in his not experiencing death, a most remarkable happening. Death cannot prevail over faith. Enoch did not see death and other believers live through death. Two final observations about coming to God arise from the study of Enoch. The one is that there must be the conviction that God exists—without that there is no possibility of coming to Him. The other concerns the character of God—He is a rewarder of those who seek Him out. There is no point in coming to God unless we are convinced that He is a God who cares.

The third of the faithful men before the Flood is Noah (v. 7). He is an outstanding example of faith because when he built the ark there was no sign of the Flood that was to come. Noah had nothing to go on except that God had conveyed His command in some way (the verb translated "warned" is often used of a communication from a deity). There was no visible evidence of what was to come. The word of God to Noah concerned "things not yet seen." And Noah was a man of faith; he was moved with "holy fear," an expression that means piety, not cowardice. This faith in action "condemned the world"; the people of the day must have asked Noah what he was doing and why. But none of them went along with him in obedience to God; when the Flood came the only ones to enter the ark were Noah and his family. The faithful obedience of the patriarch stands in sharp contrast to the attitude of the worldly. Where they were lost, he entered into the blessing. Not only did he escape a watery grave, but he became "heir" of salvation, "heir" denoting secure possession, not the entering into possession of someone's goods after the person's death. The further reference to "the righteousness that comes by faith" (more literally "the righteousness according to faith") is noteworthy as being the only example of this writer's use of "righteousness" in the Pauline sense of the "right standing" that is given to believers.

C. The Faith of Abraham and Sarah (11:8–19)

The Jews traced their descent from Abraham and honored him as the founder of their race. The Christians also honored him, but for a different reason—he was the outstanding example of a man who believed God and who lived on the basis of that faith. Thus he is seen as "the father of all who believe" (Rom. 4:11), whether they are Jews or not. Throughout the New Testament he is held in the highest esteem, an esteem shared by our author, who gives him more space than anyone else in his list. He is the classic example of what faith means. We see this when God called him to leave his country and his people to go to a land that He would show him in due course. God also promised him His blessing (Gen. 12:1–3), but that was all Abraham had to go on. He did not know what land God intended his descendants to have, but he did know what God had told him to do. He did not understand all that God had for him, but he understood obedience. So he went out, "even though he did not know where he was going" (v. 8). To leave behind the familiar certainties and to go out into the unknown with nothing to go on but the command of God—that is what faith is all about.

This faith was evident when in due course Abraham reached Canaan. We should not get the wrong impression from "he made his home" (v. 9), for the expression does not mean permanent residence. It points to the status of a resident alien, one who does not really belong and who may be required to leave at any time. Abraham had no rights and no status. He was "like a stranger in a foreign country." To the end of his life the only part of "the promised land" that he owned was the field in which Sarah was buried, and he had to pay for that (Gen. 23). Isaac and Jacob were included with him in this living in tents in the land that God had promised would be theirs. They shared in the same promise, but they had no more possession of it than Abraham did. On the human level there was nothing to justify any of these men in their trust in God. Incidentally, this is the one place in the whole Bible where we have the expression "the promised land" (literally, "the land of promise"), an expression that has been widely used, both in Christianity and beyond it.

Part of the reason for Abraham's steadfastness is that his attention was not captivated by anything earthly but by "the city with foundations" (v. 10). In the ancient world the city was seen as the center of culture, the place where most meaningful life was to be found; "city" is thus a good way of referring to the ideal existence for the people of God, and our author can look for "the heavenly Jerusalem, the city of the living God" (12:22), or "the city that is to come" (13:14), the "city" that God has prepared (v. 16). This city has "the foundations" (the Greek has the article). There are references to the foundation of the earthly Jerusalem (Ps. 87:1), while the heavenly Jerusalem has twelve foundations (Rev. 21:14). The writer is saying here that the city for which Abraham looked is the one city that has sure foundations, foundations that will last through eternity. He adds that its "architect and builder is God." The two words point to design and to actual construction: both are due to God alone. Neither word is applied to God elsewhere. The writer is saying that Abraham had a vision of what God would do. It was a vision that looked beyond Canaan, for it could equally be said of other lands that God had made them. But Abraham's "city" was clearly unique.

A very difficult problem arises because the Greek text appears to ascribe to Sarah something possible only for members of the male sex (v. 11); literally it means, "By faith also Sarah herself (being) barren received power for the depositing of semen." The NIV takes the words about Sarah as parenthetic, so that the reference to the faith of Abraham carries on from the previous verse, and also inserts the words "Abraham" and "father" to make the meaning clear, but neither is in the Greek and it is doubtful whether all this is justified. Another suggestion is that the words about Sarah be omitted, but as there is no manuscript evidence for this we should not take this line. An interesting suggestion is that we should see the words "depositing" and "semen" as symbolic, so that the meaning would be that Sarah received power for founding a line of descendants. Perhaps better than any other is the view that we should take advantage of an ambiguity in the way Greek was written in antiquity and see the critical words to mean, "By faith he, together with barren Sarah herself, received power. . . ." It is still the faith of Abraham that is in mind (and continues to be down to v. 19), but here Sarah is linked with him.

There is another difficulty in that in the Genesis account Sarah does not appear to display faith. When she heard that she was to have a child she simply did not believe it but laughed at the prospect (Gen. 18:10–15). But the writer to the Hebrews seems to be dealing, not with her initial reaction, but with her ultimate attitude. She cooperated with Abraham, which indicates that she came to share his faith. The pair were past the age when a child could have been born to them by the ordinary natural processes. But they recognized the faithfulness of God and accepted His promise. The result was that from this one man, "and he as good as dead" (v. 12), came innumerable descendants. The number of stars in the sky and the number of grains of sand on the seashore were often used in the Old Testament to indicate what is too numerous to count.

The writer has not finished with Abraham, but at this point he introduces a brief summary of what he has said so far. "All these people" (v. 13) are those he has discussed since verse 4. Characteristic of them all is the fact that when they died they still had not received all that God had promised. All through their lives they lived in faith. They did, of course, receive a partial fulfillment and it could be said, for example, that Abraham "received what was promised" (6:15). The meaning of this is that he received a preliminary fulfillment, enough for him to know that God would do what He had said. But the complete fulfillment was still future when Abraham died, as it was with all the others. As Moses saw the Promised Land but did not enter it (Deut. 3:26–28; 34:1–4), so it was with all the people in mind here: they saw enough to know that God would do as He had said, but they did not see the completion. For that they had to rely on faith. Because of their close relationship with God they saw themselves here on earth as "aliens and strangers" (v. 13; cf. Gen. 23:4; 47:9; Ps. 39:12). God's people are always pilgrims. They "are looking for a country of their own" (v. 14). They may settle for quite long periods, as Isaac and Jacob did (Gen. 26:12; 33:17), but they are never completely at home in worldly surroundings. They look for something better.

The writer brings out the point that this does not mean that they are simply looking for some other earthly place. There was nothing to stop the patriarchs from going back to the land they had left (v. 15). If their affections had really centered on Mesopotamia they could have returned. But they made no attempt to do so. It is revealing that when Abraham was giving instructions to his servant about getting a bride for Isaac from his own clan, he expressly said, "Make sure that you do not take my son back there" (Gen. 24:6). The patriarchs were not simply worldly men who left one country in the hope that they would be more successful in another. They were godly men who looked for something that could not be found in any earthly country. They "were longing for a better country—a heavenly one" (v. 16). The writer is referring to their trustful walk with God, their readiness to obey Him at all times, and the fact that the narratives clearly reveal that they valued their communion with God above all things else. They sought God, and in seeking Him they sought the heavenly country.

And God responded. There are two things: He "is not ashamed to be called their God," and He has made ready "a city" for them. Again and again God is spoken of as "the God of Abraham, the God of Isaac, and the God of Jacob" and sometimes He uses these words of Himself (Exod. 3:6, 15–16; cf. Mark 12:26–27). The writer does not say that one day God will prepare a city for them. He has already done so. And "city" in this context stands for all the blessings of the heavenly Jerusalem (cf. v. 10).

The writer returns to Abraham and draws attention to the most testing time of the patriarch's whole life, the time when he was commanded to offer his son Isaac in sacrifice. It was a test of Abraham's love for God and for his son, but it was also a test posed by what appeared to be conflicting revelations, and it is the latter that is prominent here. God had told Abraham, "It is through Isaac that your offspring will be reckoned" (v. 18; see Gen. 21:12). But God had also told Abraham to offer Isaac as a burnt offering (Gen. 22:2). How could these revelations be reconciled? Abraham was sure that both came from God, so he could deny neither. But if he could not understand he could obey. He "offered Isaac"; the Greek perfect tense indicates that as far as Abraham was concerned the sacrifice was complete. He left no doubt about his determination to do as God told him. He was in the process of sacrificing (this is better than the NIV's "was about to sacrifice"); the tense indicates that the sacrifice was not in fact completed. The writer refers to Isaac as Abraham's "one and only son" (v. 17), which we must take in the sense "unique"; there were other sons of Abraham (Gen. 25:1–2, 5–6), but none had been born in the way that Isaac was and none were the object of the kind of promises that had been given to Isaac.

Our author explains Abraham's action as proceeding from a conviction that God is able to "raise the dead" (v. 19). Even if he were to kill Isaac in accordance with God's command, that would not be the end of the matter. God could raise him and so fulfill His promise. And since Abraham had in a sense already offered Isaac (v. 17), there was a sense in which he did receive his son back from the dead. In this chapter there are many examples of people whose faith operated in a way that conquered death, and this is a striking example.

D. The Faith of the Patriarchs (11:20–22)

The writer proceeds to the faith of those who followed Abraham and emphasizes the fact that each had a faith that looked beyond death. He begins with Isaac's blessing of his sons (Gen. 27:27–29; 39–40) and the fact that the blessings referred to "their future," to things that would happen long after Isaac's death (v. 20). The patriarch spoke confidently, for he could not think that death was strong enough to defeat God's purpose. He could speak in faith, a faith that was sure of the power of God. Some find a difficulty in the fact that Isaac had been deceived and that when he blessed Jacob he thought he was blessing Esau. This is, of course, true, but it does not greatly affect the argument. Isaac speedily recognized that the blessing did in fact belong to Jacob (Gen. 27:33), and at a later time he blessed Jacob again, this time knowing full well what he was doing (Gen. 28:1–4). Our author does not go into such details. He has many people to write about and he keeps his discussion short. It was enough that Isaac spoke about the future in faith that God would act well beyond his own death. In fact, death was irrelevant. What God led His servant to say, God would do.

Jacob was another example of faith in the face of death. It was "when he was dying" (v. 21) that he blessed his grandsons (the story is in Gen. 48). There are some unexpected, even unnatural features in this blessing. Jacob treated his grandsons as if they were sons, a most unusual alteration of ranking. And further, he made the younger more important than the elder (as had happened in the case of himself and Esau). The purposes of God are worked out in God's way and are not to be confined to the way men would like to have them.

There is a further point about Jacob: the writer reminds us of his act of worship (Gen. 47:31). This took place before the blessing of the children, but the order has been reversed, in all probability to put the blessing of Ephraim and Manasseh immediately after that of Jacob and Esau, which it so closely resembled. The act of worship is relevant to the present discussion because it took place at the end of the incident in which Jacob asked Joseph to see that he was buried in Canaan, not Egypt. It was Canaan, not Egypt, that was the Promised Land, and Jacob wanted his burial to mark that fact. An interesting minor problem springs from the fact that in antiquity Hebrew was written without vowels, and the reader was required to supply them. Normally this presented no great difficulty, but now and then there is ambiguity. If we supply one set of vowels in Genesis 47:31 we get a reference to the "bed" (KJV, RSV). But those who translated the Hebrew into Greek supplied another set and got a reference to the "staff." Our author, as he usually does, follows the Septuagint and thus we have "he leaned on the top of his staff." The important thing is not that on which Jacob leaned, but the fact that he worshiped. It was this that was significant for faith.

The final member of this trio is Joseph, and his instruction that he be buried in Canaan is singled out (v. 22). Like the others, he looked beyond death and was certain of the power of God. In his case this is all the more interesting in that, after reaching the age of seventeen, he spent all his life in Egypt. But he recognized that Canaan was the land God had promised and he gave his directions accordingly (Gen. 50:24–26). Despite his riches and his place of power in Egypt he saw himself as a member of God's people and thus as one whose land was the land God had promised.

E. The Faith of Moses (11:23–28)

Moses was highly esteemed among the Jews. He had given Israel the Law, which was at the heart of the nation's religious life and the subject of diligent study on the part of its scholars. Not content with the information given in Scripture, they had surrounded Moses with all sorts of legends; clearly they held him in the highest esteem. But, in accordance with his habit throughout this chapter, our author praises him for one thing only, his faith. Actually, he begins with the faith of Moses' parents (v. 23), who disobeyed the king's command and hid their beautiful child for the first three months of his life (Exod. 2:1–2). Our Old Testament speaks only of the mother, but obviously the father was involved: the mother could not have concealed him without the father's consent. The Septuagint version has plural verbs, which indicates that both parents took part in the concealment. The reason given here is that "they saw he was no ordinary child," or better, that he "was beautiful." The beauty of the child so impressed the parents that they believed that God had something special for him to do. So they saved him, even though it meant disobedience to a royal edict (Exod. 1:22), and presumably the possibility of severe punishment. But they trusted God; it was their faith that guided their conduct, not fear of the consequences.

The writer says nothing about the finding of the baby in the papyrus basket or about the Egyptian princess taking him under her care. He goes directly to the time when Moses was a mature man and "refused to be known as the son of Pharaoh's daughter" (v. 24). We should not pass this by too quickly. Egypt was a great power and a place in the highest stratum of Egyptian society was open to Moses. Wealth and position were in his grasp. He gave it all away, and for what? "To be mistreated along with the people of God" (v. 25). By any worldly test this was a stupid decision, but it put Moses among God's people. And it has had the interesting consequence that to this day Moses is honored throughout the world, whereas the great ones who undoubtedly scoffed at his decision are completely forgotten. Even the name of Pharaoh's daughter is not known.

There is no suggestion that Moses himself was particularly badly treated when he cast in his lot with the Israelites. But they were being oppressed and he shared in the oppression. He belonged with "the people of God." His refusal to enjoy "the pleasures of sin" does not mean that he had been a dissolute character while he lived at Pharaoh's court. It means that it would have been a sin to have accepted a place in the palace with its attendant pleasures, for it would have meant disobeying the call of God. But Moses knew that the pleasures Egypt offered could be only "for a short time," and he looked farther ahead than that. His values were lasting values.

This is brought out with the comparison of "disgrace for the sake of Christ" with "the treasures of Egypt" (v. 26). The linking of Moses with Christ is unexpected. Some have understood this to mean that Moses suffered the same kind of insults as Jesus had to endure, but this does not seem to be what the author is saying. Rather, he is thinking along the lines of Isaiah: "In all their distress he too was distressed" (Isa. 63:9). God identifies with His people, so that He is one with them when they suffer. Paul had the idea of Christ's preexistence when he spoke of Him as the "rock" that accompanied Israel during the people's wilderness wanderings (1 Cor. 10:4). Our author has something of the same idea. He thinks of Jesus Christ as the same yesterday as today (13:8). Christ has always been one with God's people, and thus when Moses was insulted it was not only for God's sake, but for Christ's sake. For the writer of the epistle this is important. He is calling on his readers to stand with Christ, and it is a telling point when he can say that the great lawgiver Moses did just this so many centuries ago.

Moses had a true grasp of relative values. He knew what "the treasures of Egypt" were. He had been brought up on them and from early days no doubt was accustomed to the thought that they were his for life. But he had come to recognize that it was better to be with the people of God, even though that meant insult and suffering. Some things matter more than earthly treasure. There is a "reward" for all God's people, even though it is not the kind of reward that can be put on the scales and weighed against a heap of gold. Moses "looked away" from what he had in Egypt to what it meant to be one of God's own.

There is a minor problem associated with Moses' leaving of Egypt (v. 27), for he left twice, once when he fled to Midian and again when he went out with the nation at the Exodus. Some understand the latter to be in mind here, but this seems a strange way to refer to the departure of a whole nation. Moreover, the Passover is not mentioned until verse 28 and Moses' departure seems to take place prior to that. We should also bear in mind that the Exodus took place as the result of Pharaoh's request (Exod. 12:31–32), not his anger. All in all it seems that we should accept the meaning as the departure to Midian.

Here another problem arises: we are specifically told that "Moses was afraid" (Exod. 2:14). But we are never told that it was this fear that caused Moses to leave the country. Granted that the powerful king was opposed to him, there were other courses he might have followed. He might have hid in Egypt, or he might have headed a slaves' revolt. The author is saying that it was not fear that drove Moses from Egypt but his vision of God: "he persevered because he saw him who is invisible." That is to say, he recognized that it was not yet God's time for deliverance, so he went to Midian and waited. To view Moses' actions in this light is to see that when he went out of Egypt it was "by faith."

The Passover, with its accompanying sprinkling of blood, is a further example of faith (v. 28). At the time the first Passover was celebrated and the blood put on the doorposts, Pharaoh had given no indication that he was ready to let the Israelites go. To prepare for departure was an act of faith. So was Moses' instruction to keep the Passover throughout succeeding generations (Exod. 12:14, 17). It showed a profound faith when, after nine successive plagues had not shaken Pharaoh's determination, at least not to the point of his letting the people go, Moses prevailed on the entire nation to keep the Passover and to put the blood on the doorposts. And his faith was vindicated, for the destroyer passed over the firstborn of Israel. Let the readers take heart from the example of this great leader.

F. The Faith of the Exodus Generation (11:29–31)

We do not normally remember the Exodus generation as shining examples of faith. We remember their constant complaints to Moses and their disobedience, which meant that in the end almost all of them perished in the wilderness. But the writer is not giving a full account of all that happened. For example, he does not mention Joshua, who was certainly a fine example of a man of faith. He is making a selection that will bring out his point that faith has always been the way for the people of God. And it took faith for the Israelites to pass through the Red Sea. How could they be certain that the waters would not come back and destroy them? The way the people of this world reason, they could not—their certainty was the certainty of faith. Because they believed they went forward and treated the path through the sea as "dry land" (v. 29). But it was not an obvious and easy way for the worldly: when the Egyptians tried to do the same thing they were drowned. Faith was necessary for the safe passage through the sea. Undoubtedly the Egyptians were courageous men, but courage is not enough; it is a valuable part of life, but it can never be a substitute for faith.

The writer passes over the years in the wilderness and comes to the first striking success in the conquest of Canaan, the falling of the walls of Jericho (v. 30). All that the people did was march around the city in silence, the priests blowing their trumpets, until the great moment when they all shouted and the walls came down (Josh. 6:1–21). From the worldly point of view, nothing could have been more pointless than simply to march around the city. But from the standpoint of faith it was the only thing to do. God had commanded and the people of God had to obey. When they did, their faith was vindicated.

Rahab (v. 31) is at first sight an unlikely candidate for an outstanding example of faith. But she certainly was ready to risk everything for her conviction that "the LORD your God is God in heaven above and on the earth below" (Josh. 2:11). Had her compatriots in Jericho known what she was doing, they would certainly have put her to death. She risked everything for her convictions about the God of Israel, and her faith was vindicated. The other inhabitants of the city are called "disobedient" (or possibly, "unbelieving"). The point is that they had heard as much about God's dealings with Israel as Rahab (Josh. 2:10). But where she came to recognize that God is the God of heaven and earth and came to trust Him, they did not. They continued on their worldly way and suffered inevitable destruction. We might add that Rahab became an ancestress of our Lord (Matt. 1:5) and that James commends her (James 2:25). She was highly esteemed among the Jews and was accounted as one of the four most beautiful women (the others being Sarah, Abigail, and Esther). But for our author the one thing that matters is her faith.

G. The Faith of Other Servants of God (11:32–38)

The writer cannot go on indefinitely pointing out what men and women of faith have accomplished; there are simply too many of them. So he says just that, and proceeds to a generalizing summary. If he cannot go into detail he can point to the kind of thing that happened over and over. He lists half a dozen Old Testament characters in an order that has puzzled commentators. It is not chronological; if we arrange them in pairs, the second in each case is earlier than the first. Nor is it in ascending or descending importance. We can say that it is natural to have Samuel last, for he was the first of the prophets and leads naturally into a reference to the prophets generally. But no convincing reason has been given for the order of the others. The first four are mentioned only here in the New Testament, and Samuel but twice elsewhere, though David, of course, is mentioned often. People of faith are not necessarily on everyone's lips, but they are important nonetheless.

No specific deeds of the men named are given, but each battled against such great difficulties that from the purely worldly point of view he had little chance of success. But they were faithful and God honored them. That does not mean that they were in all points worthy examples to be followed. Calvin pointed out that Gideon was slow to act, and that Barak also hesitated; in fact, he went forward only when Deborah stood by him, and that in a day when women had no role at all in military matters. Samson, of course, was led astray by Delilah, while Jephthah was foolish in the vow he made and stubborn in the way he kept it. This leads Calvin to say, "In every saint there is always to be found something reprehensible. Nevertheless although faith may be imperfect and incomplete it does not cease to be approved by God." We should not take the list of the heroes of the past as a source of discouragement when we think of our own shortcomings. The great ones also had defects, but that did not stop them from living by faith. Nor should it stop us.

The expression "by faith," which has been characteristic of this chapter up till now (with an occasional "according to faith" in the Greek), is now replaced with "through faith," although there does not appear to be any great difference in meaning (v. 33). It is still trust in God that matters. The list begins with "conquered kingdoms," which could certainly be said of Joshua and indeed the others in the list just given. This is followed by "administered justice," an expression that fits people like the judges; it may have a wider application, but the judges form a useful illustration of the scope of the term. Some understand the words as "did deeds of righteousness," which is a possible way of taking the Greek. It would then apply to almost any act of Christian service, but this is probably too wide. People like the judges seem more likely to be in mind. The third group are those who "gained what was promised" (NIV), or possibly those who "received promises" from God (RSV). Either way they were people who had faith. The man who comes to mind when we read of shutting the mouths of lions is, of course, Daniel, though we should bear in mind that Samson, David, and Benaiah were also delivered from lions (Judg. 14:5–6; 1 Sam. 17:34–37; 1 Chron. 11:22).

Those who "quenched the fury of the flames" (v. 34) remind us of Daniel's companions whom Nebuchadnezzar consigned to the fire and who were so signally delivered (Dan. 3:19–27). Others "escaped the edge of the sword," which may refer to people in situations like that of Elijah, whom Jezebel sought to kill but who was delivered (1 Kings 19:2–8). People "whose weakness was turned to strength" abound in the Old Testament and for that matter in the New. It is one of the basic features of serving God that He supplies those with little strength with whatever strength is needed (cf. Deut. 33:25). This was seen, for example, in the victories won by Gideon's three hundred (Judg. 7:7), and by Ahab's armies that were "like two small flocks of goats" (1 Kings 20:27). God's strength is never limited by human weakness.

Now the writer turns to troubles associated with persecutions and the like (v. 35), although the first item on his list might include, e.g., the women whose sons were raised from the dead by Elijah and Elisha (1 Kings 17:17–24; 2 Kings 4:18–37). Nor should we forget that Jesus raised the son of the widow of Nain (Luke 7:11–14) and His friend Lazarus (John 11). There was also Dorcas, who was brought back from death to life when Peter prayed (Acts 9:36–41). The readers had a number of examples to encourage them.

But we must not think that the Christian way is a kind of insurance policy, so that those who believe are freed from all the troubles of life. God is powerful enough to deliver His people from every adversity, even to raise them from the dead, but there are occasions when in His wisdom He sees fit to allow them to undergo all manner of hardships. They glorify Him in deliverance, but they may also glorify Him in the way they endure hardship. So the writer goes on to speak of people who were tortured, a fate that has all too often befallen the people of God. Those who refused release with a view to "a better resurrection" are like some of those who suffered during the Maccabean troubles. There is a moving story in 2 Maccabees of seven brothers who were executed in turn after each had been tortured in the endeavor to make him apostatize and take part in heathen sacrifice. Their mother was enlisted to urge them to turn from the God of Israel, but instead she encouraged them to persist with words like these, addressed to the last of the seven, "Accept death, so that in God's mercy I may get you back again with your brothers" (2 Macc. 7:29).

A lesser torment faced some who had to put up with "jeers and flogging," while others endured chains and imprisonment (v. 36). We should not underestimate the suffering involved in this. For example, the word used here for "jeers" is used in the incident of the seven brothers just mentioned. When the second brother was brought forward, the "jeers" took the form of tearing the skin and the hair from the young man's head (2 Macc. 7:7). The cognate verb is likewise used of the torture and death of the third brother (2 Macc. 7:10). Flogging was carried out with a whip of many strands, the leather thongs of which were loaded with pieces of bone or metal. It was a brutal punishment and in some cases resulted in death.

With "stoning" (v. 37) we come to a characteristically Jewish form of execution. The writer is probably reminding the readers that some Christians had suffered at the hands of their fellow countrymen (cf. the stoning of Stephen, Acts 7:57–60). There was a tradition that the prophet Isaiah had been executed by being sawn in two, but this was certainly a most unusual way of killing anyone. Being put to death by the sword was much more widespread. It is important that this be included in the list, so that people should not gather from the deliverances mentioned (particularly that in v. 34) that God's people were always safe. If they held this belief they were likely to be discouraged the moment they saw someone suffering or being executed for being a Christian. The writer is saying that God's grace is sufficient for any need. If God's purpose is deliverance, no force on earth can resist it. But if in His providence any of His servants is to suffer, then that servant will be given grace to glorify God in and through suffering.

Typically, the people of God have lived simply, and the writer speaks of them as clothed in sheepskins and goatskins (v. 37). We are reminded of Elijah (2 Kings 1:8), while Zechariah refers to "a prophet's garment of hair" (Zech. 13:4). John the Baptist wore a garment of camel's hair (Mark 1:6). It seems that this kind of clothing was recognized as suitable for a man of God. The reference here is to others than prophets, but the language conjures up recollections of the ways of the prophets and of the suitability of simple clothing for God's people. With this goes the fact that they were "destitute"; those in mind were completely without worldly wealth. The writer is speaking of people whose circumstances of utter poverty and continual ill-treatment and persecution singled them out as totally miserable in the world's eyes.

But that shows how wrong the world is. The world "was not worthy of them" (v. 38). Despite their outward circumstances they were infinitely better off than the world because they were the people of God and in receipt of the blessing of God. But the writer does not dwell on their blessedness. He goes on to speak of their lack of proper housing. They wandered in lonely places far from the haunts of men. They lived in caves ("holes in the ground" are underground caves). The whole passage speaks of the reversal of values that follows when one puts one's trust in God. The comforts and pleasures of worldliness are then seen for the shallow things they are. The people of God may be poor and despised, but their faith provides them with riches the like of which the world has never known.

H. The Promise (11:39–40)

The writer rounds off his treatment of the great men and women of faith in former days with the interesting information that, despite all they had done for God and all the blessings they had received, they would not enter into the final blessing apart from the Christians. There is a strongly social aspect to God's dealings with people. We belong together in the church of God, and while there is rich blessing indeed for the believer in lonely places, the fullness of God's blessing comes only in company with all God's people. Paul prayed that the Ephesians might "have power, together with all the saints, to grasp how wide and long and high and deep is the love of Christ" (Eph. 3:18) and there is something of the same thought here. The nature of the final blessing of God is such that we can know it only "with all the saints."

So the writer speaks of the heroes he has listed as having testimony borne to them (NIV, "were commended") "for their faith." His "all" is important—not one of them is forgotten. But for all the testimony borne to them, not one of them received "what had been promised." In a sense, of course, they did receive "what was promised" (v. 33) and Abraham has been singled out because he "received what was promised" (6:15). We should bear in mind that there are many promises of God and that His servants continually see fulfillments of what God has said He will do for them. The author is not denying any of this; his words are very explicit. But he distinguishes between the blessings God gives His people along the way and the final blessing. It was this final blessing that they did not receive; indeed, in God's plan they could not, for that blessing involves all the people of God. We should also understand it to involve the saving work of Christ, which is the decisive thing that has been before us throughout this epistle. Without it there could be no final blessing. Only through what Christ has done can any of God's people be "made perfect."

For Further Study

1. What differences do you see between faith as Paul writes about it and faith as we see it in Hebrews 11?
2. What do we learn about the nature of faith from the opening statements of this chapter?
3. Consider Abraham. Why does the author give more space to him than to any of the other heroes of faith? What may we learn from the faith of this great man?
4. Find five things taught us by the faith of Moses.
5. Throughout this chapter there is a strong emphasis on the importance of trusting God for the future. What examples of this can you find?

Chapter 10

Christian Living

(Hebrews 12:1–13:19)

The writer has given attention to great Christian truths. He has put emphasis on the finality of what God has done in Christ. He has made it clear that Christ is to be seen as greater by far than anyone in all creation and as having perfectly accomplished by His death what the animal sacrifices could not do. He has pointed out that what God looks for is faith and that He has always looked for faith. But he does not think that the way Christian people live is unimportant, and at the end of his letter he gives attention to this.

A. Christ Our Example (12:1–3)

He has emphasized the fact that Christ has brought about our salvation by His death. This is an objective fact, something that Jesus has done quite apart from us. But now he reminds us that not only is Jesus our Savior, He is also our example. While it would be a total misunderstanding of the author's argument to see any possibility of adding to the perfection of what Christ has done, it is still true that believers are to work out the implications of their salvation. The redeemed of the Lord must live as such.

The writer begins with the fact that "we are surrounded by such a great cloud of witnesses" (v. 1). There is dispute among expositors whether we should understand these witnesses to be those who are witnessing us in our earthly struggle and pilgrimage, or whether they are those who have witnessed to the faith by which they lived and to the God they delighted to serve. The word used of them is *martus*, from which we get our word "martyr"; a martyr is one who witnesses to the faith. Thus it would be quite natural for the writer to follow up chapter 11 by reminding his readers that there is a multitude of witnesses to the faith. In favor of this it is also urged that the word does not mean "a spectator." All this may be granted, but it is difficult to rid the passage of the thought that the witnesses witness us as well as having borne their witness to God in the days of their flesh. It is not easy to see why they are said to surround us, if we are simply urged to think of them. It is also true that in some passages the idea of "spectator" is hard to eliminate from the word used. Thus Paul writes of Timothy's "good confession in the presence of many witnesses" (1 Tim. 6:12). This meaning seems also to be involved in our author's reference to certain sinners as being executed "on the testimony of two or three witnesses" (10:28). Furthermore, we should bear in mind that the readers are exhorted to look at Jesus (v. 2), not the giants of the faith. All in all, it seems that the author includes the idea here that the heroes of the faith are aware of what we are doing as we maintain the struggle in our age that they had in theirs. It is something like a relay race where those who have completed their run watch their successors.

This is all the more possible in that the imagery of a race certainly pervades the rest of the verse. We should carry no surplus weight that would hinder us in running (in the first century runners in competition ran naked). There are things that are not wrong in themselves but that hinder us from being the best we can be in Christ's service. We must jettison them. And, of course, we should be rid of sin. The word translated "that so easily entangles" is a most unusual one, found nowhere else. But its form makes it clear that it means "easily surrounding" and hence "easily entangling." The writer is saying that sin is a hindrance to the Christian athlete, so he must put it away decisively. And he must persevere in running the race so that he runs it to the end. The metaphor is not that of a short sprint, but of a distance race. It is a race that is to be run throughout our lives.

We are to look away from all else and "fix our eyes on Jesus" (v. 2); He is our inspiration and it is to Him that we run. He is "the author and perfecter" of faith (the NIV inserts "our," but the word is lacking in the Greek). The word "author" is also used in 2:10, where we noted that it might mean a leader or one who does a thing first; it may "emphasize authorship, leadership, or priority." Some take it in the sense of "going first" in this passage (cf. RSV, "pioneer"); the thought then would be that Jesus lived by faith and thus showed us the way. He saw His task through to the end and is accordingly the "perfecter" of faith. This is certainly a possible understanding of the text. The NIV takes it to mean that Jesus began the work of faith in us and that He will see it through to completion. There is truth in both approaches.

The expression rendered "for the joy set before him" is ambiguous. The Greek preposition *anti* ("for" in the English versions) often has the meaning "instead of," "in the place of," and many take it in this sense here. If this is right, the author is saying that Jesus gave up the joy that He saw before Him, the joy of bliss in heaven; He abandoned it in order to go to the cross for our salvation. But *anti* may also mean "for the sake of" (as it does in the expression "*for* this reason," Eph. 5:31), and if we understand the word in this way the author is saying that Jesus looked beyond the cross. He endured it because of the joy that bringing salvation to sinners meant. It seems that it is this second meaning that we should adopt here. With this joy before Him Jesus put up with all the suffering that crucifixion brings and scorned the shame of the cross. In the Roman world, crucifixion was regarded as the most shameful of deaths, and no matter how terrible his crime, a Roman citizen could never be crucified. But Jesus was not deterred by such considerations. Crucifixion was the way by which salvation was to be won, so He accepted its pain and its shame. They meant nothing to Him in the light of the joy of bringing salvation. And having this work of bringing salvation completed, Jesus sat down in the place of honor "at the right hand of the throne of God."

The readers are invited to let their consideration of what Jesus has done for them inspire them to continue the struggle (v. 3). "Consider" translates a word used of making calculations: "Work it out for yourselves" is the force of it. The opposition they were experiencing from evil people was not something new and unique. Jesus had endured it all before and with His example before them they should go on to the end. The athletic metaphor is carried on in the words rendered "grow weary" and "lose heart." Both are used of runners who have put forth their best effort and, after they have crossed the finish line, relax and collapse. The readers have not yet completed their course. Their race is still being run. They must not give way to weariness or discouragement.

B. Discipline (12:4–11)

In this life there is a good deal of meaningless suffering. When a tyrant tortures a helpless prisoner there is no meaning in it and it is desperately hard to bear. But there is also suffering that is meaningful, childbirth for example. The pain is real pain, but the fact that it is meaningful, that it will result in the birth of the baby, puts it on a different level from torture. Our author does not gloss over the suffering that lay in the path of his friends, but he points out that, for the Christian, suffering has been transformed: it is still painful, but it has meaning. The cross shows that it is suffering that brings us salvation; and Jesus called on His own to take up their cross and to do it daily (Luke 9:23). The writer here makes the point that there is such a thing as disciplinary suffering and believers must be ready to recognize and accept such suffering. It will help to advance the purposes of God and it will make them better people.

We easily interpret an expression like "struggle against sin" (v. 4) as referring to temptation; we feel the temptation and struggle against it. But, whether we overcome it or give way to it, this struggle does not involve the shedding of blood. The writer is surely referring to a different struggle, the struggle the readers were having against the sin of powerful oppressors. He is reminding them that that struggle has not yet proved fatal for any of them. They should not exaggerate its seriousness. He does not minimize it: his "not yet" implies that it was possible that some would lose their lives. But their situation was not as difficult as that faced by other Christians. Let them keep their sense of proportion.

He recalls them to a passage in the Bible they were in danger of overlooking, a passage that reminds the readers that discipline awaits every son (vv. 5–6). He quotes Proverbs 3:11–12 and calls it "that word of encouragement." We do not usually think of a promise of suffering as an encouragement, but the writer is saying that disciplinary suffering is inseparable from sonship. The father who really cares for his son will discipline the boy as part of his training for life. The person who sees God as Father will recognize a similar thing in the happenings of life. The reader is not to "make light of the Lord's discipline," as though the sufferings of life could be dismissed as mere chance or the like. Nor should the believer "lose heart"; these difficulties are evidence, not that he is going to be defeated by troubles he cannot overcome, but that God loves him. The writer puts the words "because whom he loves" first in the clause for emphasis. If God did not care about us He would not bother to discipline us. The writer sees in life's sufferings the evidence of the love of God that uses hardship as a means of making us the best that we can be. "Everyone he accepts as a son" must expect discipline. Perhaps we should notice that this would have been more obvious in the ancient world than in modern western communities. The father had absolute rights within the family and it was expected that he would punish. Modern permissive attitudes had no place. The readers would accept the inevitability of punishment in any well-ordered household.

It is possible that we should take the word translated "Endure hardship" (v. 7) as a statement, not a command. Thus the RSV renders, "It is for discipline that you have to endure." The important thing, though, is not whether we have a command or a statement (either would suit the context), but the emphasis on the words "as discipline." They come first in the sentence and they are important. For the Christian, suffering is not simply sheer misery, nor is it the result of blind chance. It is fatherly discipline. It takes place because "God is treating you as sons." The point is important for our author and he brings it out in a variety of ways. This makes sense, for it is clear that the readers were suffering, and it is not easy for sufferers to see any value in their sufferings. They are always ready to reject well-meant advice and concentrate on their misery. But the author is sure of the validity and the importance of what he is saying, so he keeps hammering away at it. It was impossible for him (and for that matter for his readers) to think of a loving father who did not discipline his sons.

What if someone is not disciplined? This shows that he is not a son (v. 8). Illegitimate children were not on the same footing as the legitimate; they were not part of the family, they were not heirs. They were not disciplined in the same way as sons, and this was not something they could be happy about. It showed that they were outside the sphere of the father's caring. Suffering is not to be treated lightly.

The writer appeals to what had in fact happened in the families to which he and his readers belonged (v. 9). They had all had fathers. They had all been chastised. And what was the result? They respected their fathers. No one would dream of seeing in the discipline imposed by an earthly father mere wanton cruelty. The respect they had for their fathers ruled such a thing out entirely. We should not have less respect when we experience discipline at the hands of the heavenly Father; rather, we should submit to Him and thus have life. Our lives will always be impoverished if we do not see suffering in a proper light. It is certain that we will undergo hardship and difficulty. If we are always rebelling against it and refusing to learn the lessons the Father is teaching us, we are shutting ourselves up to discontent and misunderstanding. To live life to the full means to accept our sufferings, to see meaning in our sufferings as well as in our joys. "The Father of our spirits" is a very unusual expression, found only here in the Bible (though Num. 16:22; 27:16 are similar). Some think the reference is to "the spirits of righteous men made perfect" (v. 23), and indeed God is the Father of such. Others see a reference to all mankind. There is no "our" in the Greek, so the expression is not necessarily limited to Christians. But perhaps the best way to understand the expression is to take "of spirits" as equivalent to the adjective "spiritual." A number of translations have "our spiritual Father" (e.g., TEV, NEB, JB).

The writer continues with what our earthly fathers have done (v. 10). They certainly disciplined us, but there were two limitations on what they did. One was that of time: they did it "for a little while," i.e., during the days of childhood. This, of course, contrasts with the life-long discipline God's people receive at His hands. The other limitation arises from the limited knowledge of those earthly fathers. They disciplined us "as they thought best," but their best was imperfect—they inevitably made mistakes. But God's discipline is always "for our good." His perfect knowledge and His perfect power over all the circumstances of life make it certain that what happens to us is ultimately for good (cf. Rom. 8:28). We can be sure of God's discipline, far more sure than we can be of that of our earthly parents to whom the writer makes such confident appeal. He adds a comment about the end result of God's discipline. It is "that we may share in his holiness," which reminds us that God's character is not limited by sin like that of all of us here on earth, and that God's aim in our salvation is that we should come to share in something of that holiness. The end result in salvation is not that we should be left much as we were at the beginning but that we should be remade in the likeness of our God.

The writer rounds off this section of his argument with the reminder that there is a difference between receiving discipline and the later savoring of the end result of it all (v. 11). Suffering is never pleasant. No one likes it. All the glib talking in the world cannot gloss over the fact that we naturally shrink from pain. But if it is accepted in the right spirit "it produces a harvest of righteousness and peace." We expect "righteousness"; that is an obvious aim for disciplinary chastisement. But "peace" is not so obvious, and indeed, it has not been as evident as we would like among Christians through the centuries. Even the martyrs who laid down their lives for the faith have sometimes been people so sure of the rightness of their cause that they have been ready to quarrel with others who did not see things their way. Suffering must be borne in the right spirit if it is to lead to peace. And this is not simply a matter of natural temperament; it comes to "those who have been trained by it." The metaphor from athletics is continued with the reminder that training is necessary for a good performance. So the Christian submits to training in discipline and accepts a way of life that leads to peace.

C. Exhortation to Live the Christian Life (12:12–17)

Because God is active in fatherly discipline ("Therefore") the writer sees it as important that the readers respond. He speaks of "feeble arms and weak knees" that should be strengthened. The word is actually "hands" rather than "arms," and the combination gives the impression of someone whose four limbs are all ineffectual (cf. Isa. 35:3). But this paralysis can and must be put right. Most understand "make level paths" (v. 13) as "make straight paths" (RSV). Not only are the limbs paralyzed, but the paths are also imperfect and the readers are to put them in order. This will help the lame, the feeble members of the church, and with a change of metaphor, the writer looks for them to be healed. Strong Christians have a responsibility to help the weak and it is this that is being urged at this point. It is important that the church be at its best, and this means that every member should function at the peak of perfection.

This involves among other things the pursuit of peace and holiness (v. 14). It is the way of the world to be self-assertive, which makes for friction and disharmony. It is the way of Christ's people to be peaceable (Matt. 5:9; Mark 9:50; Rom. 12:18), a state that does not come about by drifting aimlessly. It requires "every effort," and the readers are to make that effort. They are also to pursue the holiness without which no one will see the Lord. Holiness is the state of being separated to belong to God; Christians do not simply accept the world's ways and the world's standards. While they play their full part in the community to which they belong, Christians do not live by worldly standards. They are God's servants and their attachment to God shows in the standards of conduct they adopt.

This does not mean that their own strenuous efforts produce results.

They are to make full use of "the grace of God" (v. 15); unfortunately, God's people do not always use the resources God provides (cf. 2 Cor. 6:1; Gal. 5:4). The readers are also to see that no "bitter root" grows up (cf. Deut. 29:18). The metaphor from plant life brings out the point that bitterness may be slow in growing, but if the seed has been sown the plant is inevitable in due time. And its effects are widespread; in the end bitterness will "defile many." It makes them unfit for the presence of God.

A third danger is being like Esau (vv. 16, 17). There is no evidence that this man was sexually immoral (though some take the reference to be to his Hittite wives, Gen. 26:34). But he was an irreligious man, one given to indulging his appetites, as is manifest in his selling of his birthright for one meal (Gen. 25:29–34), and the two may well be taken together. The readers are being warned against making the gratification of bodily appetites the central thing in life. Nothing is known of Esau's change of mind other than what we read here, but the writer appeals to the readers' knowledge of it, so evidently it was common knowledge at the time. Evidently, in due course Esau came to see that he had been foolish and wished to reverse his decision. But he found that it could not be done. It is important to take care before committing ourselves to worldly decisions, for sometimes they cannot be reversed. Esau had been very emotional about it and clearly very much in earnest. But he could not go back. We should be clear that this is not a matter of forgiveness of sin. Esau could have repented and found God's forgiveness for his wrongdoing. But he could not undo what he had done.

D. Mount Sinai and Mount Zion (12:18–24)

The writer takes his contrast between Judaism and Christianity a stage further with a comparison between Mount Sinai and Mount Zion. He does not refer explicitly to Mount Sinai or even to a mountain (despite the NIV). He keeps his reference general, speaking of "what may be touched. . . ." There is no doubt that he refers to what happened on Mount Sinai (cf. Deut. 4:11), but he chooses to put it this way to bring out the outward and the material which were such important features of what he is opposing. For "the trumpet blast" (v. 19), see Exodus 19:16, 19; 20:18. The "voice speaking words" reminds us that God spoke on that occasion (Deut. 5:24) and the people were terrified (Exod. 20:19; Deut. 5:25–27). The awe-inspiring nature of the events is emphasized in the command that not even an animal must touch the mountain (v. 20; cf. Exod. 19:13); stoning (or the use of darts or arrows in Exod. 19:13) could be inflicted without touching the mountain. Its holiness must be maintained.

The effect of it all was that even Moses, who lived so close to God, was terrified (v. 21). The words quoted come from the incident of the golden calf (Deut. 9:19). He may have used the words on both occasions, or the writer may simply be reasoning that, since everyone was afraid (Exod. 20:18), Moses was included. It is also possible that he is taking words Moses undoubtedly spoke on one occasion and applying them to the same man on a similarly terrifying occasion. God was present, but His presence, under the old way, meant fear.

But Christians, by contrast, are not subject to an experience like that at Sinai (v. 22). Basically, Christianity is concerned not with terror but with joy. Zion was one of the hills on which Jerusalem was built and it sometimes stands for the home of God's people, as does, of course, "the heavenly Jerusalem" (cf. Gal. 4:26; Rev. 3:12; 21:2, 10). We have already had references to God's city (11:10, 16), and it is now seen as "the city of the living God." The impression given is that of a dynamic, joyous affair, and this is further brought out with the multitude of angels "in joyful assembly."

The impression of joy is carried on with "the church of the firstborn" (v. 23), though the exact meaning is not as clear as we would like. Some take it to refer to the angels just mentioned, but angels are not commonly called a church, nor are their names said to be written in heaven as are those of believers (Luke 10:20; Rev. 21:27). But it is hard to see the expression as meaning the church in heaven, which is surely in mind later: "the spirits of righteous men made perfect" (v. 23). And it is hard to see it as the church on earth, for the readers are said to come to this group and how could they come to that of which they are members? The writer is perhaps referring to the whole church in heaven and on earth and thinking of the readers as having come *into* it, not simply *to* it.

He proceeds with a reference to God as Judge of all, which in this context points to His vindication of "the spirits of righteous men made perfect." They are where they are and in the condition they are only because of what God has done. We do not often have a reference to the departed saints as "spirits"; the expression perhaps is meant to bring out the fact that in the end it is the spiritual that matters.

And they have come to Jesus (v. 24). He is here described with reference to the new covenant that is so central for the writer. The covenant associated with Mount Sinai has been replaced by that of which Jesus is the Mediator. He shed His blood for it and that blood says something far better than did the blood of Abel. Abel's blood cried out for the punishment of the killer (Gen. 4:10). Jesus' blood cleanses the conscience of sinners (9:14) and brings them into the very presence of God (10:19).

E. A Kingdom That Cannot Be Shaken (12:25–29)

This section concludes with a contrast between things that can be shaken and things that cannot; obviously the readers will do well to concentrate on the permanent. First, they should not "refuse" the God who speaks. From his first sentence, the writer has insisted that God spoke to

Israel from of old, but throughout his epistle he is equally insistent that Israel has not responded to that word from God as it should have done. He urges his readers not to make the same mistake with the fuller revelation they have in Christ. The revelation at Sinai was a revelation made "on earth," and as the Old Testament says again and again, Israel refused to live by that revelation. The warning for Christians is plain: they have received even more than Israel had and consequently have a greater responsibility.

The point is driven home with a reminder of the way the earth shook at Sinai (v. 26; cf. Exod. 19:18; Judg. 5:4–5; Ps. 68:8, etc.) and the prophecy that there will be one more shaking that will include heaven as well as earth (Hag. 2:6). The end of this world will be much more significant than what took place at Sinai. The writer draws special attention to the words "once more" (v. 27), for they point to more than merely one shaking among others: this is a once-for-all shaking, a shaking that will end the merely earthly. It will separate the things that "can be shaken" from those that cannot. That is to say, it will mean the end of this creation. It is important, accordingly, to give serious attention to those things that will remain after the shaking.

Believers are to live in thankfulness, for they receive "a kingdom that cannot be shaken" (v. 28). We should probably take the words, "let us be thankful," in the sense "let us hold on to the grace that we have been given" (JB). Elsewhere in this epistle the word *charis* always means "grace," and though it is true that it can be used of gratitude, it is more likely that we have here an exhortation to hold on to grace as we worship God. It is only by grace that we can approach Him. The word for "worship," incidentally, often has the wider meaning "serve" (KJV) and that may be what is in mind. Any aspect of Christian service, whether it be worship or any other, must be undertaken in a proper spirit, "with reverence and awe." The writer adds a reason—"our God is a consuming fire" (v. 29; cf. Deut. 4:24). Real love is concerned to destroy everything that is evil in the beloved. This is what distinguishes love from sentimentality. Christians must always rejoice in being loved by God, but that should not make them complacent. There is still such a thing as the wrath of God.

F. Love (13:1–6)

In living the Christian life nothing is more important than love. It is this that is characteristic of the followers of Jesus (John 13:34–35). There is a special love they have for one another, and the readers are urged to practice this brotherly love (*philadelphia*, v. 1). But they should also practice love in a broader sphere, and the writer immediately goes on to the way they should treat "strangers" (v. 2; cf. Gen. 18–19). Happy and unexpected results may follow hospitality.

A particular outworking of love concerns prisoners (v. 3). As we have noted before, in antiquity prisoners had a particularly hard lot and it was important that God's people have compassion on such. The readers should sympathize with prisoners and with "those who are mistreated" as if they themselves shared the same fate (as well they might in due course under the conditions of first-century life!). There was little that prisoners could do to alleviate their lot, so it was important that Christians take what action they could to help.

From this outworking of love for others the writer turns to love in marriage (v. 4). In the first-century Roman empire, marriage was held in low esteem and there was widespread immorality. The Jews and the Christians stood out with their concern for sexual purity and this is an example of it. We should probably take the opening words as an imperative, not simply as a statement of fact: "Let marriage be held in honor among all" (RSV). The writer is urging the readers to act rightly within the marriage bond. He is probably also rejecting the position of some ascetics who objected to marriage and the sex act on principle. "The marriage bed" is a euphemism for sexual intercourse, so the author is advocating both the married state and the use of sex within marriage (notice that he characterizes the latter as "pure"). The other side of this coin is the rejection of adultery and fornication, both of which come under the judgment of God.

Another false love is the love of money (v. 5), which the poor among us cannot dismiss as simply the vice of the rich. It is concerned with an attitude toward possessions and not with the amount, though of course riches provide a temptation. In an affluent society it is easy to be caught up in the continual pursuit of possessions; where the love of money is, people can never have enough. The writer wants his readers to learn that "enough is enough." In any case, the continuing endeavor to get more money is needless, for God has promised never to leave His people, which means that they will always be provided for (cf. Matt. 6:25–33). The writer quotes Scripture, but the words do not exactly come from any passage, though they agree with what is said in several (e.g., Gen. 28:15; Deut. 31:6; Josh. 1:5, and others). The Jewish philosopher Philo has this quotation in identical words (he does not say where it is from), which raises the possibility that both are quoting from a Greek translation that no longer exists. Be that as it may, the writer emphasizes the importance of depending on God, not money. He has a second quotation (v. 6), this time one we can identify (Ps. 118:6–7). Such passages from the Bible give confidence. God will provide for His people; they should not burden themselves with worry.

G. Christian Leadership (13:7–8)

We do not know enough about the organization of the church in the first century to know precisely who are in mind in the reference to "your leaders" (v. 7). They may have been elders, but we do not know for certain. What is important is that they should be remembered and imitated. It has always been easy to be critical of leaders. They are in exposed positions and there are always flaws. But the value of their work should be recognized. These are people who "spoke the word of God," an expression that means the whole Christian message. They should be held in honor accordingly.

The verb "spoke" is in the past tense and this, taken in conjunction with the reference to "the outcome" of their way of life makes it likely that the writer is referring to past leaders rather than present ones. It is not impossible to see a reference to current leadership, but it is more likely that those of an earlier day are in mind. But it is surely going too far to see a reference to the deaths of martyrs, as some suggest. What the writer is speaking of is the whole way of life of men who lived in faith. That is something for which the readers should be thankful and which they should imitate.

Notice once again the reference to faith. That is of central importance and leads on to one of the great statements about Jesus Christ, the object of faith. The writer uses the full name "Jesus Christ" but rarely (only here and in 10:10; 13:21); it brings dignity and solemnity to the statement. "Yesterday and today and forever" gathers up all time, past, present, and future, into an emphatic expression of Christ's changelessness. His eternal being never changes and accordingly His followers may rely on Him. The writer has looked at past leadership, but Jesus Christ goes back farther. His present reality gives confidence, while "forever" looks as far as one can look into whatever ages lie ahead. It matters not which way we look, He is the same. If we are thinking of Christian leadership we are thinking of Christ as our great Leader.

H. Christian Sacrifice (13:9–16)

In the religions of antiquity the act of animal sacrifice was the central act of worship, but the Christians stood apart from this. When they gathered for worship they never offered an animal. But this does not mean that they were indifferent to all that is caught up in the word "sacrifice." As the writer has made clear already, this term spoke to Christians of the sacrifice Christ offered once and for all. He now comes back to the theme, this time in the context of the temptations that must have been encountered by Christians to conform their way of worship to what was universal in other religions.

He begins with a warning against "strange teachings" (v. 9). The word "strange" is really "foreign"; here it means "foreign to the gospel." The reference to foods points to the problem of clean and unclean foods (which was a distinction made by almost all religions), or to the use of meat from animals that had been offered in sacrifice. People from other religions would insist that there was merit in eating certain foods. They perhaps argued that these foods strengthened the hearts of the worshipers, i.e., sustained their inner life. The writer contradicts this. It is "by grace" that our hearts are sustained; ceremonial foods are "of no value." Those who walk in the ways of such religions are not profited.

This leads to a consideration of the "altar" (v. 10). Christians had no altar in their place of worship and this may have been a reproach thrown at them. The writer maintains that in fact they do have an altar. An altar points to sacrifice and Christians point to the cross, the place where the one sacrifice that can put away sins was offered. That is an altar in a much more meaningful sense than the pile of stones used by adherents of other religions. Others, and specifically "those who minister at the tabernacle," have no rights in the cross. They do not come to it in faith and thus cannot "eat" there, i.e., partake in all that it means.

The Day of Atonement ceremonies come to mind at this point. The writer has already used some features of the observance of this day to bring out truths such as Jesus' winning for His own access to the very presence of God (10:19–22). Now he is concerned with a very different aspect. While the blood of the sacrificial animals was solemnly manipulated in "the Most Holy Place" (v. 11) the disposal of their bodies was a very different matter. The carcases could not be eaten, as was the case with other sacrifices. They must be taken outside the camp and burned there (Lev. 16:27).

The expression "outside the camp" leads to two important thoughts. The first is that Jesus died "outside the city gate" (v. 12). His death did not fit into the Jewish system in any way. It was foreign. It was "outside." But it was the way whereby Jesus made the people "holy." He cleansed them from their sin and set them apart to belong to God. He did this "through his own blood," i.e., His death. It was the fact that He died as He did, died the death of a criminal on a cross, a death completely outside all that "the camp" of Judaism could embrace, that brought salvation. Let the readers be clear that salvation does not come from what took place within the camp—it came from the death outside the camp.

The other thought is that because of what Christ has done believers should themselves "go to him outside the camp" (v. 13). To be Christians meant putting themselves outside the camp of Judaism. So be it, then. Christ had died a shameful death for them outside the camp; it was right that they should link themselves with Him outside the camp. It meant "bearing the disgrace he bore," but this has always been the fate of God's people. It may be significant that this same word "disgrace" has been used of Moses (11:26) who suffered "disgrace for the sake of Christ." The writer is saying that a break with Judaism is necessary. That will mean reproach and the like. The Jews will look down on them for associating themselves with Jesus. But the way of the true servants of God (like Moses) has never been easy or popular. In one way or another it has always involved a going outside the camp.

As he has done before, the writer points his readers to the "city" in which they are interested, not an earthly city belonging to the here and now, but "the city that is to come" (cf. 11:10, 16; 12:22). The city stands for the best in community life, and the writer is saying that the best is not here on earth. Believers have a place in the earthly city where they live, but this is not "enduring." It lasts for but a short time. Their values are eternal values and they must wait for the realization of all that means. They look for "the city that is to come." The verb the NIV translates "are looking for" denotes a wholehearted search. The writer is not speaking of a casual glance but of a thoroughgoing concentration on the search.

Which brings us to the thought that there is in fact a "sacrifice" that Christians offer. They may have no physical altar in their places of worship, but that does not mean that they do not know what sacrifice means, nor that they do not offer sacrifice. Sacrifice means the death of Christ to bring an effective salvation, and an effective salvation means not only forgiveness but transformed lives. It means continually offering to God "a sacrifice of praise" (v. 15). This is not something that people do spontaneously and of themselves; it is "through Jesus." This is stated with some emphasis and it rules out the Jewish way, or for that matter, any other. Jesus is the one way to God, the one person through whom we may offer worship acceptably. This is done "continually" (cf. 1 Thess. 5:18), which may be meant in contrast to praise offered at set times in Judaism. "The fruit of lips that confess his name" is a reference to Hosea 14:2, where the prophet rejects worship that is merely external and calls for deep and sincere repentance.

With words go deeds (v. 16). It is not enough to say the right words; believers must also do the right deeds. This is first put generally: they are "to do good," which covers a whole way of life. Then specifically, they are "to share with others," a duty Christians can never escape, not least in a world with vast gaps between the affluent and the poor. The writer makes the point that it is things of this nature that form the kind of sacrifice with which God is pleased.

I. Christian Obedience (13:17)

There has already been a reference to Christian leaders (v. 7), probably those of an earlier time. Now the readers are exhorted to take up a proper attitude toward current leadership. Leaders can never do their job unless followers play their part. Followers must accept the fact that they are followers and give due obedience to those in places of responsibility. How else can the leaders get their work done? Then we read of the essential work of the leaders: they "keep watch over you." More literally, the Greek means "they keep watch over your souls" and it is a question whether translations like the NIV and NEB are correct in taking "your souls" as equivalent to "you." There is a lot to be said for following the KJV and RSV; we would then take the reference to the souls as indicating the essential sphere of responsibility of the leaders. Their basic concern is the spiritual welfare of those who are subjected to their leadership.

The leaders are not autocrats with absolute rights over the rank and file. They are responsible people "who must give an account." Church people should bear this in mind and help the leaders by following their directions. Then the work of the leaders will be "a joy, not a burden." All too often leaders must put up with a kind of passive resistance that makes all their work difficult. By contrast, some congregations make work a joy for their leaders as the Thessalonians did for Paul (1 Thess. 2:20; cf. also Phil. 2:16; 3 John 4). Apart from other considerations, there is no advantage to a congregation in resisting leaders. It is in their own interest as well as in that of the leaders that they give them full support.

J. Prayer (13:18–19)

One way in which followers can support leaders is by praying for them and the writer appeals to the readers to pray for him. The reference to his being "restored" to them shows that he had at one time been with them, and the general tone indicates that it had been as a leader. Now he wants their continual prayers: "keep praying" is the force of the present imperative. The NIV omits the word "for" ("for we are sure . . ."), which gives the reason for the request for prayer. "That we have a clear conscience" is a very unusual reason for looking for prayer support, and it may indicate that the readers had at some time accused the writer of some misdeed, perhaps of being away from them for some inadequate reason. Whatever it was, he protests his innocence and makes this the reason why he can expect them to pray for him.

There is a transition from "we" to "I," which some take to mean that the writer is associating other people with him at first, but then moves to a personal request. This is possible, but it seems more likely that "we" is no more than a literary plural and that the whole small paragraph is concerned only with the writer and the readers. The writer has not linked others with him previously in the letter and there seems no reason why he should do it here. Incidentally, such a transition from plural to singular is found also in other places (cf. Gal. 1:8–9; Col. 4:3).

The prayer that he may be restored to the readers shows that the writer was in some difficulty. It has been suggested that he may have been in prison. This is possible, but there is no evidence and it is just as possible that the obstacle was something like sickness. We simply do not know. Whatever it was, it was outside the control of the writer and he wants prayer so that it may be overcome.

Chapter 11

Conclusion
(Hebrews 13:20–25)

A. Doxology (13:20–21)

The letter closes with a wonderful doxology, which has meant much to generations of Christians, followed by some greetings. The doxology (vv. 20–21) speaks of "the God of peace" (cf. Rom. 15:33; 16:20; 2 Cor. 13:11; Phil. 4:9; 1 Thess. 5:23), which may be meant to remind the readers that real peace does not consist in relapsing to Judaism but in a right relationship to God. It is He who brings the blessing of peace, the well-rounded prosperity of the whole personality.

This is the one place in the epistle where the Resurrection is mentioned. As is usual in the New Testament, it is seen as due to the action of the Father (occasionally it is said that Jesus "rose," but it is much more common to say that the Father "raised" Him). The doxology brings in the saving work of Christ and links the Father with it. Jesus is "that great Shepherd," but the Father raised Him "through the blood of the eternal covenant." These are two ways of saying that it is in what Christ has done in dying and rising that the needs of mankind are met. That the shed blood of Christ is the way the new covenant is established has been brought out earlier (e.g., 9:15). Now is added the thought that the God of peace was involved in it as well. And the link with the Resurrection points to the truth that it is not a dead Christ who is in mind, but One who triumphed over death.

Jesus is "that great Shepherd of the sheep" (cf. Isa. 63:11; John 10:1–18, where the Shepherd theme and resurrection are connected; 1 Peter 2:25). This reminds us of the helplessness of believers, for sheep are in desperate straits without the care of the shepherd. And it emphasizes the tender care that Christ brings His own, providing for their every need.

The prayer is that God will "equip" the readers with all that they need, so that they may do the will of God. To do that will is never a purely human achievement; it requires a work of grace within. The writer looks for God to supply what is needed. He goes on to a fascinating statement of the interplay of the divine and the human in Christian service. It is human, for we are to be "doing" God's will; our effort is involved. But it is divine, for the prayer goes on, "may he work in us . . ."; it is God who does the work. Neither aspect should be overlooked. Nor should we fail to notice the plural "we." The writer associates himself with the readers in all this; he does not set himself on a pedestal. He, just as much as they, needs the help of God.

The doxology concludes with an ascription of glory to God or to Christ. There seems no compelling reason for limiting it to either. Doxologies refer mostly to God and He is the subject of the main verb. But on the other hand, "Jesus Christ" comes immediately before the words in question. The writer probably is not trying to distinguish between them. Glory belongs to both, and that "for ever and ever." Doxologies normally end with "Amen," which is a mite unexpected, for the word was the response of a congregation to something said by its leader. Evidently it was so much a matter of course that it came to be included with the doxology.

B. Final Exhortations (13:22–25)

The writer refers to his letter as "my word of exhortation" (v. 22), which is very similar to the description of a sermon in Acts 13:15 (where "encouragement" is the translation of the word rendered "exhortation" here). The writer sees his letter as like a sermon. He remembers that he has had some hard things to say of the readers and he appeals to them now to take them all in the right spirit, an appeal that is reinforced with the affectionate address, "Brothers." It is perhaps curious that he speaks of his letter as "short," for it is a fairly long letter compared to many that have come down to us from antiquity. But the subjects he has dealt with are such that it would have been possible to write on them at much greater length (even a modest commentary like this is much longer!). The letter is short in comparison with what its subject matter might have demanded.

There is a slight ambiguity in the reference to Timothy (v. 23). The verb might be an imperative ("Know ye," KJV), or a statement ("You have no doubt heard"), but probably the former. The general impression the passage leaves is that the writer is giving information, not repeating what is known. There seems no reason for seeing Timothy as anyone other than Paul's companion (no other Timothy is known to us from the early church). Evidently he had been in prison but had now been set free. It would seem that he had warm relations with both the writer and the readers: he is "our brother," and it is expected that he and the writer will come to visit the readers.

The greetings sent to "all your leaders" (v. 24) show that the letter was sent neither to the whole church nor to its officials. They show also that there was nothing underhand about it; the readers would pass on a message to the leaders. This is the third mention of the leaders in this chapter; clearly they were very important to the writer. Greetings go also to "all God's people," or more exactly, "all the saints." "The saints" are those set apart, those who belong to God. Exactly opposite conclusions have been drawn from the words "Those from Italy." Some hold that the letter was written from Italy, and that the local Christians sent their greetings; others see it as evidence that the letter was written from some other place and that the Italian Christians who were there sent greetings to the recipients (who were presumably somewhere in Italy). The question must remain unresolved.

The writer concludes by praying for grace for all his readers. This is the normal way of ending a New Testament letter, and it has a special suitability in a letter like this, which emphasizes so strongly what God had done in Christ, but which also indicates that the readers were in some spiritual need. "Grace" is both a reminder and a promise.

For Further Study

1. How does a contemplation of the "great cloud of witnesses" help us in our Christian service today? What are some of the things we should "throw off" (12:1)?
2. In what ways does the writer help us with the problem of suffering?
3. What lessons may we learn from Esau? From Abel? From the scene at Mount Sinai when the Law was given?
4. What does this passage teach us about the working of love in the life of the believer?
5. "Sacrifice" is a term with many meanings. What significance does it have for Christians?
6. Make a list of things we can learn from chapter 13 about Christian leaders.

Bibliography

Barclay, W. *The Letter to the Hebrews.* Edinburgh: Saint Andrew, 1955.

Bowman, J. W. *Hebrews, James, I and II Peter.* London: SCM, 1962.

Brown, J. *An Exposition of Hebrews.* 1862. Reprint. London: Banner of Truth, 1961.

Bruce, F. F. *The Epistle to the Hebrews.* Grand Rapids: Eerdmans, 1964.

Buchanan, G. W. *To the Hebrews.* New York: Doubleday, 1972.

Calvin, J. *The Epistle of Paul the Apostle to the Hebrews and the First and Second Epistles of St. Peter.* Edinburgh: Oliver and Boyd, 1963.

Delitzsch, F. *Commentary on the Epistle to the Hebrews.* 1871. Reprint. Minneapolis: Klock & Klock, 1978.

DuBose, W. P. *High Priesthood and Sacrifice.* London: Longmans, 1908.

Héring, J. *The Epistle to the Hebrews.* London: Epworth, 1970.

Hewitt, T. *The Epistle to the Hebrews.* London: Tyndale, 1960.

Kent, H. A. *The Epistle to the Hebrews.* Grand Rapids: Baker, 1972.

Loane, M. L. *Key-Texts in the Epistle to the Hebrews.* London: Marshall, Morgan & Scott, 1961.

Manson, W. *The Epistle to the Hebrews.* London: Hodder & Stoughton, 1951.

Moffatt, J. *A Critical and Exegetical Commentary on the Epistle to the Hebrews.* Edinburgh: T. & T. Clark, 1913.

Montefiore, H. W. *A Commentary on the Epistle to the Hebrews.* London: Black, 1964.

Nairne, A. *The Epistle of Priesthood.* Edinburgh: T. & T. Clark, 1913.

Pfitzner, V. C. *Chi Rho Commentary on Hebrews.* Adelaide: Lutheran Publishing House, 1979.

Purdy, A. C. *The Epistle to the Hebrews.* New York: Abingdon, 1955.

Robinson, T. H. *The Epistle to the Hebrews.* London: Hodder & Stoughton, 1933.
Scott, E. F. *The Epistle to the Hebrews.* Edinburgh: T. & T. Clark, 1922.
Snell, A. *New and Living Way.* London: Faith, 1959.
Spicq, C. *L'Épître aux Hébreux.* Paris: Gabalda, 1952.
Tasker, R. V. G. *The Gospel in the Epistle to the Hebrews.* London: Tyndale, 1950.
Westcott, B. F. *The Epistle to the Hebrews.* London: Macmillan, 1892.
Williamson, R. *Philo and the Epistle to the Hebrews.* Leiden: Brill, 1970.

BIBLE DICTIONARIES AND ENCYCLOPEDIAS

Buttrick, G. A., ed. *The Interpreter's Dictionary of the Bible.* 4 vols. New York/Nashville: Abingdon, 1962.
Hillyer, N., Rev. ed. *The Illustrated Bible Dictionary.* 3 vols. London: Inter-Varsity, 1980.
Orr, J., ed. *The International Standard Bible Encyclopedia.* 5 vols. Grand Rapids: Eerdmans reprint 1957. Revision, ed. G. W. Bromiley, 4 vols. 1979–.
Tenney, M. C., ed. *The Zondervan Pictorial Bible Dictionary.* Rev. ed. Grand Rapids: Zondervan, 1967.
———. *The Zondervan Pictorial Encyclopedia of the Bible.* 5 vols. Grand Rapids: Zondervan, 1975.